A Manifesto for Social Progress
Ideas for a Better Society

At this time when many have lost hope amid conflicts, terrorism, environmental destruction, economic inequality, and the breakdown of democracy, this beautifully written book outlines how to rethink and reform our key institutions – markets, corporations, welfare policies, democratic processes, and transnational governance – to create better societies based on core principles of human dignity, sustainability, and justice. This new vision is based on the findings of over 300 social scientists involved in the collaborative, interdisciplinary International Panel on Social Progress. Relying on state-of-the-art scholarship, these social scientists reviewed the desirability and possibility of all relevant forms of long-term social change, explored current challenges, and synthesized their knowledge on the principles, possibilities, and methods for improving the main institutions of modern societies. Their common finding is that a better society is indeed possible, its contours can be broadly described, and all we need is to gather forces toward realizing this vision.

MARC FLEURBAEY is an economist, professor at Princeton University (Woodrow Wilson School and Center for Human Values) and member of Collège d'Etudes Mondiales (Paris FMSH). He is the co-author of *Beyond GDP* (with Didier Blanchet, Cambridge University Press, 2013), *A Theory of Fairness and Social Welfare* (with François Maniquet, Cambridge University Press, 2011), and the author of *Fairness, Responsibility and Welfare* (2008). He was a coordinating lead author for the IPCC 5th Report, and one of the initiators of the International Panel on Social Progress. He is also a member of the UN Committee on Development Policy, and of the Council for Global Problem-Solving.

OLIVIER BOUIN is an economist, director of the RFIEA Foundation, which supports Institutes for Advanced Study in France, Europe and worldwide, and former director of the Collège d'Etudes Mondiales (FMSH, Paris). His research interests focus on institutional economics, European economics and international science policies. He is the co-editor of *Europe's Crises* (with Manuel Castells et al., 2018). He is a member of the Governing Board of the European Alliance for Social Sciences and Humanities, and one of the initiators of the International Panel on Social Progress.

MARIE-LAURE SALLES-DJELIC is a sociologist, professor, and dean of the School of Management and Innovation at Sciences Po. Her research focuses on the interface between business and society – the historical transformation of capitalism, the cross-national diffusion of ideas and practices, business ethics and corporate social responsibility, transnational governance, and the performative role of ideologies. She has published broadly on these issues in academic journals and books. In particular, she is the author of *Exporting the American Model* (1998), winner of the 2000 Max Weber Award (American Sociological Association) and, together with Sigrid Quack, of *Transnational Communities: Shaping Global Governance* (Cambridge University Press, 2010).

RAVI KANBUR is an economist and professor at Cornell University. He has served on the senior staff of the World Bank including as chief economist for Africa. He is president of the Human Development and Capabilities Association, chair of the Board of United Nations University-World Institute for Development Economics Research, a member of the OECD High Level Expert Group on the Measurement of Economic Performance, former president of the Society for the Study of Economic Inequality, a past member of the High Level Advisory Council of the Climate Justice Dialogue, and a past member of the Core Group of the Commission on Global Poverty.

HELGA NOWOTNY is professor emerita of Social Studies of Science, ETH Zurich, and former president of the European Research Council (ERC). Currently she is chair of the ERA Council Forum Austria and visiting professor at Nanyang Technological University, Singapore. Her active engagement in scientific boards includes the Walling Falls Foundation (member), Lindau Nobel Laureate meetings (vice-president), and Complexity Science Hub Vienna (chair), among others. Her latest book publications are *The Cunning of Uncertainty* (2015) and *An Orderly Mess* (2017).

ELISA REIS is a political sociology professor at the Federal University of Rio de Janeiro and chair of the Interdisciplinary Network for Social Inequalities Studies (NIED). Her research focuses on elite perceptions of poverty and inequality, and on contemporary changes in the patterns of interaction between state, market, and society. She has published widely in Brazilian and foreign periodicals. She is one of the authors of the book by Michele Lamont et al., *Getting Respect, Responding to Stigma and Discrimination in the United States, Brazil and Israel* (2016).

A Manifesto for Social Progress

Ideas for a Better Society

MARC FLEURBAEY

with

OLIVIER BOUIN, MARIE-LAURE
SALLES-DJELIC, RAVI KANBUR,
HELGA NOWOTNY, AND ELISA REIS

CAMBRIDGE
UNIVERSITY PRESS

CAMBRIDGE
UNIVERSITY PRESS

University Printing House, Cambridge CB2 8BS, United Kingdom

One Liberty Plaza, 20th Floor, New York, NY 10006, USA

477 Williamstown Road, Port Melbourne, VIC 3207, Australia

314–321, 3rd Floor, Plot 3, Splendor Forum, Jasola District Centre,
New Delhi – 110025, India

79 Anson Road, #06-04/06, Singapore 079906

Cambridge University Press is part of the University of Cambridge.

It furthers the University's mission by disseminating knowledge in the pursuit of
education, learning, and research at the highest international levels of excellence.

www.cambridge.org
Information on this title: www.cambridge.org/9781108424783
DOI: 10.1017/9781108344128

© Cambridge University Press 2018

First published 2018
Reprinted 2018

Printed in the United Kingdom by TJ International Ltd. Padstow Cornwall

A catalogue record for this publication is available from the British Library.

Library of Congress Cataloging-in-Publication Data
Names: Fleurbaey, Marc, author. | Bouin, Olivier, author.
Title: A manifesto for social progress : ideas for a better society / Marc
Fleurbaey, Princeton University, New Jersey, Olivier Bouin, Paris.
Description: Cambridge, United Kingdom ; New York, NY : Cambridge
University Press, 2018. | Includes bibliographical references and index.
Identifiers: LCCN 2018015099 | ISBN 9781108424783 (hardback)
Subjects: LCSH: Social policy. | Economic policy. | Equality. | Democracy.
Classification: LCC HN18.3 .F548 2018 | DDC 306–dc23
LC record available at https://lccn.loc.gov/2018015099

ISBN 978-1-108-42478-3 Hardback
ISBN 978-1-108-44092-9 Paperback

Contents

v

Foreword

Amartya Sen

Can social justice be cultivated? Can social progress be enhanced through dedicated research and its application? This manifesto – with its powerful vision and practical recommendations – draws on individual and collaborative research of more than 300 social scientists. The investigative findings have been put together with clarity and force by a team led by Marc Fleurbaey.

If the epistemic message underlying the Communist Manifesto published 170 years ago was the diagnosis that "the history of all hitherto existing society is the history of class struggles," the main message of this manifesto of social progress is that justice can certainly be cultivated and social progress can be substantially enhanced through combining a constructive vision with well-thought-out changes in institutions and conventions. In contemporary debates on political economy too much time may have been spent already arguing for *or* against the market economy. We need to move on to the recognition that market institutions are necessary but far from sufficient as the basis of a just society – a society that guarantees fairness and human dignity as well as sustainability and robustness. Contemporary capitalism goes beyond making use of the market economy – often with uncritical application – by enforcing certain priorities and exclusions, all of which are open to questioning and careful scrutiny. It is such questioning and scrutiny that identifies, in this manifesto, the institutional and behavioral changes that just social progress demands.

It would be a mistake to think that the need for a manifesto of this kind has arisen only from the recent manifestations of inequity and fragility that the world sees today. As Adam Smith noted more than two centuries ago, the market economy needed – even then – both support and skepticism. He argued for allowing the markets to function in normal circumstances, but also for organizing institutions that restrain counterproductive market activities of "prodigals and projectors," and that allow the state to do those essential things that the state alone can best perform. If such a balance was necessary in the eighteenth century at the dawn of modern capitalism, it is totally essential in the prosperous and yet unjust world in which we live today.

I very much hope that this manifesto, based on findings of extensive research, will generate initiatives that will be able to change the face of the globe. Radical changes are needed in the stricken and unjust world in which we live, and there are good reasons to think that the positive vision and constructive proposals presented in this manifesto will greatly contribute to that much-needed transformation. It is hard to exaggerate the global importance of a far-reaching manifesto of this kind.

Preface

The recent decades have seen a decline in world poverty and an extension of democracy in many countries around the world. Nevertheless, many people have the feeling that this has also been a period of social setbacks, and there is a general atmosphere of skepticism regarding the possibility of long-term substantial social progress, not to mention a deeper transformation overturning the prevailing social injustices. Most intellectuals shy away not only from utopian thinking, but from any long-term prospective analysis of social structures. The crisis of social democracy after the collapse of the Soviet empire seems, in the West, to have generated a decline of hope for a just society just as the conditions of life of hundreds of millions of people in emerging economies have dramatically improved. These countries, however, have also abandoned the search for a different path to development: the trend is now to mimic the developed countries, rather than inventing a new model, and social hardships reminiscent of the early phase of Western capitalism are widespread in these countries.

Yet neither the collapse of illusions nor booming capitalism in developing countries should mean the end of the quest for justice. Given their special competence, social scientists ought to think about the transformation of society, together with scholars from the humanities and the hard sciences. If hope for progress is possible, they should provide it. If it is not possible, they should explain why.

Paradoxically, social scientists have never been so well equipped to assume such a responsibility, thanks to the development of all the relevant disciplines since the Second World War. But the expansion of disciplines, their growing specialization, and the globalization of academic production have made it impossible for even the brightest mind to grasp, on its own, the complexity of social mechanisms and make serious proposals for changes in institutions and social structures. Such a task must now be collective and it must be cross-disciplinary.

INTERNATIONAL PANEL ON SOCIAL PROGRESS

The IPSP – www.ipsp.org – was developed to address this task. It brought together more than 300 academics (of all relevant disciplines, perspectives, and regions of the world) willing and able to engage in a true interdisciplinary dialogue on key dimensions of social progress. Relying on state-of-the-art scholarship, these social scientists reviewed the desirability and possibility of all relevant forms of long-term social change, explored current challenges, and synthesized their knowledge on the principles, possibilities, and methods for improving the main institutions of modern societies.

The Panel is a truly collaborative effort, in its organization as well as its multi-sourced funding. It seeks to work in a way that is true to the key values and principles underlying its mission: wellbeing and freedom, security and solidarity, as well as pluralism and inclusion, distributive justice and equity, environmental preservation, transparency, and democracy.[1] The group has produced a major three-volume report – *Rethinking Society for the 21st Century* – which covers the main socio-economic, political, and cultural dimensions of social progress, and explores the values, the opportunities, and the constraints that underlie cutting-edge knowledge on possible improvements of institutions and policies. The report covers global as well as regional issues and considers the future of different parts of the world – the diversity of challenges and their interplay.

---

[1] A detailed discussion of values and principles of social progress is provided in IPSP (2018a, chapter 2).

All chapters in the IPSP report focus on a particular set of issues from the double perspective of gaining insights about (1) what are currently the main risks and challenges and (2) how institutions and policies can be improved if the plagues of inequality, segregation, intolerance, exclusion, and violence are to be fought. The full table of contents and authors can be found in the appendix to this book.

THE PURPOSE OF THIS BOOK

This book is written for a wider audience to share the message of hope of the larger report: *A better society is indeed possible, its contours can be broadly described, and all we need is to gather forces toward realizing this vision*. Although it largely relies on the report, it is complementary and offers its own original perspective in a coherent analysis. It does not seek to summarize the report with all its wealth of topics, and it does not pretend to reflect the full diversity of views of the Panel members. It is an invitation to take these issues to heart and to explore them more deeply with the help of the full report.

The team who wrote this book was at the core of the work of the IPSP, and is made up of scholars who are committed both to scientific research and to making social science serve the common good:

- Olivier Bouin, General Secretary of the European Network of Institutes for Advanced Studies, former Director of Collège d'Etudes Mondiales (FMSH, Paris)
- Marie-Laure Salles-Djelic, Professor and Co-Director of the School of Management, Sciences-Po, Paris
- Marc Fleurbaey, R.E. Kuenne Professor in Economics and Humanistic Studies, Princeton University, and member of Collège d'Etudes Mondiales (FMSH, Paris)
- Ravi Kanbur, T.H. Lee Professor of World Affairs, International Professor of Applied Economics, and Professor of Economics, Cornell University

- Helga Nowotny, Professor Emerita of Science and Technology Studies, ETH Zurich, and former President of the European Research Council
- Elisa Reis, Professor of Sociology, Universidade Federal do Rio de Janeiro

Readers are invited to follow the work, watch the videos, and attend the public events of IPSP. All information is available at www.ipsp.org and on YouTube, Facebook, and Twitter.

Acknowledgments

Many people have helped in the process of making this book and deserve special thanks. Excellent research assistance has been provided by Damien Capelle, Brian Jabarian, and Flora Vourch. Ottmar Edenhofer provided very helpful advice on the taxation of carbon and rents, as well as Jean-Paul Vallée on grassroots initiatives. Comments have been generously provided at various stages of preparation of the text by Nico Cloete, David de la Croix, Fernando Filgueira, Nancy Folbre, Jeff Hearn, Nora Lustig, Wolfgang Lutz, Anne Monier, Fabian Muniesa, Gian Paolo Rossini, Saskia Sassen, Erik Schokkaert, Simon Schwarzman, Noah Scovronick, Greg Shaffer, Christiane Spiel, Alexander Stingl, Lorraine Talbot, Peter Wallensteen, Finn Wölm, and three anonymous reviewers. The institutions that have supported the whole IPSP project deserve grateful acknowledgment here as well, and especially the Center for Human Values at Princeton University, the Collège d'Etudes Mondiales (FMSH, Paris), and the Institute for Futures Studies (Stockholm), among more than thirty. Last but not least, the support of the Cambridge University Press team (in particular Karen Maloney, Stephen Acerra, Adam Hooper, Gail Welsh and Kristina Deusch) has been very important in bringing this project to fruition jointly with the larger report.

Introduction: The Future is in Our Hands

Many people these days have lost hope in the future and believe that the next generation will be worse off. Not only do they see difficulties mounting in daily life, but they no longer believe in the ideologies that offered promises for the future and inspired social and political movements in the twentieth century. Communism has lost its soul in the Gulag and nowhere now, not even in China, does it keep alive the dream of a radically different, much better society. Libertarian ideas have resurfaced under the "neoliberal" label and have been very influential in the last decades in many countries, until the Great Recession shook many observers' faith in the free market.

The death of ideologies should be welcomed. It offers a window of opportunity to shed the old dogmas and rethink the way forward. After the devastating contest between communism and freewheeling capitalism, what can we invent? This window of opportunity is also, it seems, the last chance to adjust our thought and action before looming catastrophes erupt in the form of a breakdown of social and ecological systems. This book is animated by a sense of urgency and gravity. Researchers,[1] citizens, change-makers, we all have a responsibility to live up to the challenges of our times and find solutions before the accumulated problems turn into vital crises.

This introductory chapter summarizes the key messages and main narrative of the book. It clarifies our conception of social progress and it exposes a few of the common errors in the conventional wisdom of our times that must be dispelled to clear the way for better thinking. The hurried reader will get the key takeaways by reading it.

---

[1] See IPSP (2018c, chapter 22) for an overview of how policy-making has been influenced by ideas coming from social sciences.

WHAT IS SOCIAL PROGRESS?

This book is written by researchers but it goes beyond presenting facts and science. It takes positions in the debate about the direction that policies and change-makers should take, because under some basic assumptions of what a good society would be, there are some clear dos and don'ts, and some promising ideas to explore and experiment with.

The core idea of a good society starts from the idea that every human being is entitled to full dignity, irrespective of gender, race, religion, education, talent, and productive abilities. This ideal of dignity includes the possibility to participate in social life on an equal footing with others and to be in control of the important dimensions of one's life. While equal dignity is sometimes viewed as a very minimal notion, we follow the United Nations Agenda 2030 and its associated Sustainable Development Goals (SDGs) and understand dignity as a powerful word with substantial practical implications. In fact, whenever structural inequalities in social relations appear, dignity is endangered. If you observe society around you and ask yourself "Does everyone really have equal dignity?" you will see repeated instances of unequal dignity following from gross or subtle inequalities in status, resources, and power.

Since the effort to build a better society should be wide and inclusive, this book does not commit to a precise theory of social justice, and it retains values and principles that can be accommodated in most cultures of the world. One must admit, however, that the ideal of equal dignity clashes with certain conceptions that give genders, ethnic groups, or people with different sexual orientation a different level of inclusion and dignity. If you believe that the role of women is to serve their husbands and raise their children, that there is a natural hierarchy of races, or that homosexuals are inferior or repugnant, this book will clash with your views. If you believe that equal dignity is fine but that every community should keep its purity and avoid migrations and miscegenation, this book will also go against your views because it places the dignity and flourishing of the person above the preservation of groups or nations – while trying to avoid narrow forms of individualism.

The key values and principles underlying this book include wellbeing and freedom, security and solidarity, as well as pluralism and toleration, distributive justice and equity, environmental preservation, transparency, and democracy.[2] Any project that would severely crush one of these values and principles is considered objectionable here.

FALSE IDEAS AND COMMON MISTAKES

It is not expected that every reader will be fully convinced by the arguments of this book, but hopefully every reader should feel compelled to shed a few elements of conventional wisdom that imprison people's minds nowadays and have become serious obstacles on the road to a better society.

The first false idea that must be confronted was popularized by Margaret Thatcher, who vigorously promoted a free-market agenda: "There is no alternative" (TINA). It was also disseminated through Fukuyama's (1992) "End-of-History" thesis, according to which liberal democracy and the capitalist system were the final touch to human achievements. It is ironic that this idea was pushed by Thatcher, a policy-maker who made important strategic policy moves with long-term transformational consequences. Actually, there are many possibilities in front of us for the future, even without innovating or experimenting with new ideas. There are many variants of capitalism already in place, and some are much better than others at promoting human flourishing. The TINA thesis is deceptively attractive because it builds on the blatant failure of the socialist alternatives that have been tried in the former USSR, in China, and in former Yugoslavia. It indeed contains a grain of truth: there is

---

[2] A detailed discussion of values and principles of social progress is provided in IPSP (2018a, chapter 2).

no alternative that does not include a central role for the market as an economic mechanism (with proper safeguards). The big mistake, though, is to believe that keeping a role for market transactions means adopting unfettered capitalism. In fact, as many thinkers have argued over the generations, the market *is* compatible with the idea that people should dominate things rather than the other way around. Labor can hire capital, rather than be hired by and serve capital. In this sense, this book even argues that a market economy need not be part of a capitalist society. Thus, many more alternatives than the current variants of capitalism become possible. In fact, they are already experimented with here and there, and can be scaled up. In summary, two false ideas, not just one, have been identified here: (1) that there is no alternative to the current system – in fact there is not even *a* current system, but many variants around the world; (2) that the market economy and capitalism are the same thing and that endorsing the former implies accepting the latter – in fact the market is needed but capitalism can be transcended.

A related false, pernicious idea that is especially widespread in the media is that traditional social causes have been replaced by more complex and more elusive contestations of the status quo, relating to cultural and identity problems or to environmental crises and no longer generating massive social and political conflicts. This mistake is due to the confusion between the decline of particular movements and the seeming disappearance of the underlying social problems, and is influenced by the idea that if there is no alternative, then all the movements pushing for alternatives have become irrelevant and can simply be ignored. So, let this be clear once and for all: the task of liberating women, workers, and various ethnic groups from their secular state of subordination is not finished. The task of bringing disabled people to full inclusion is also unfinished. So is the integration of migrants with a cultural background that differs from that of their new community. These traditional causes remain essential and as urgent as ever. It is true that the plight of LGBTQI people has recently risen up in our collective conscience and deserves to be added to this list, and it is definitely true that the devastation of ecosystems and other species has reached a scale that calls for urgent action. The recent rise of the #MeToo movement against the sexual harassment of women has led to a critical moment of epiphany across many cultures and continents. But, all in all, the complacency of pundits about traditional social suffering is unconscionable.

Another false but widespread idea is that salvation comes from politics and from changing government policy. Most people think that there is either too much or too little government intervention in the economy and society, and that the main solution to our current predicaments consists in changing that. What this book argues is that, in the long run, societal changes are initiated by much deeper layers of society, through transformations of methods and conventions, norms and habits, and governmental policy often comes later to stabilize and coordinate the new normal. Therefore, while the political game remains important, it is by no means the only way to hope for change and to work for it. One does not have to become a politician or a political activist to be a change-maker.

There are many other false ideas that will be attacked in this book – for instance, that technological progress follows a deterministic path that we cannot influence, that globalization implies convergence of economies and clashes of civilizations, or that social progress requires economic growth accompanied by environmental destruction. We will deal with them in due course in the following chapters.

NARRATIVE

In a nutshell, here is the story that this book tells. The advent of the Anthropocene, i.e. a new geological epoch where the main driver of change for the planet is human activity,[3] puts humanity

---

[3] The Anthropocene is still a debated idea, and some would suggest it started as early as the beginning of agriculture more than 10,000 years ago, or as recently as the first nuclear explosion during the Second World War. But the term very well captures the idea that humanity now has a great responsibility.

in the driving seat of the planet, and we collectively become aware that if we continue like this we will go over a cliff because several key tensions will burst out into cataclysms. Inequalities and lack of social cohesion are becoming unbearable across continents and within countries, generating conflicts, migrations, social unrest, and political instability; environmental degradation is reaching planetary scale, with a changing and more volatile climate and the serious risk of a new mass extinction.

The Western idea that the liberal democratic capitalist institutions have reached their final form and represent the ultimate goal (the "end of history") for all nations of the world must be firmly rejected. Achievements in social policies and democratic institutions can be swept away in one election's stroke and replaced with authoritarian and socially and environmentally destructive policies. History continues, and we need to explore new institutions to guarantee social and environmental sustainability. There are interesting ideas and innovations on all continents that can lead to new forms of popular participation, greater harmony with nature, or more effective management of conflicts. All over the world, a great diversity of economic, political, and social developments show the power of imagination and a striking range of ideas that promise a better society.

The challenge for our time is to find ways to simultaneously achieve *equity* (leaving no one behind, both inter- and intranationally, creating an inclusive society), *freedom* (economic and political, including the rule of law, human rights, and extensive democratic rights), and *environmental sustainability* (preserving the ecosystem not only for the future generations of human beings but also for its own sake, if we want to respect all forms of life). Freedom is understood here in a comprehensive way, which includes not only human rights and individual integrity, but also the right to participate in collective decisions in a democratic way, enjoying rights of free speech and association, and receiving adequate training and knowledge for full participation. Freedom and democracy are therefore inseparable and should not be opposed. Democracy can suppress freedom only when democratic institutions are ill conceived and badly implemented.

Globalization and technological innovation are key drivers of socio-economic transformations. Experts (not always decision-makers, unfortunately) know the virtues and dangers of the former, but there is much uncertainty about how the latter will affect quality of life and social inequalities. An important point is that globalization and technological innovation are not natural processes that societies must either endure or stop. Quite to the contrary, the particular ways in which globalization and innovation unfold can be shaped by policies and it is important to steer them in the direction of social inclusion. Therefore, not only should we make sure to support those who lose from the globalized economy and technological disruptions and ease their adaptation and transition to the new opportunities offered by these developments, but we can work to make the changes themselves occur in a way that generates less loss and more gain for all.

Another important factor of change is the cultural shift that expands the "circle of respect and dignity," i.e. the set of people, lifestyles, and living beings that are treated with due respect and dignity (equal dignity in the case of all human beings, including full participation in all relevant decision bodies; for non-human living beings, respect and dignity are harder to put under the equality ideal, but remain nevertheless relevant values). This seems a universal and irreversible trend, despite many setbacks and resistances. This trend, which includes an expansion in the endorsement of democratic values, is a very promising element of the better society that must now be imagined.

How can one imagine a better set of institutions and policies? It would be dramatically insufficient to envision social progress in terms of seizing the central political power in order to implement social and economic policies from above. Instead, one must address the inequalities in resources, but also and most importantly of power and status, that pervade all institutions, organizations, and groups, from the family to the transnational corporation, from the local community to the regional group of governments, from the local NGO to the political party. Reforming all these institutions and organizations in the economy, in politics, and in social life will not happen simply by making more "progressive" parties come to government, but will involve grassroots initiatives and changes in the governance of many organizations, in particular and crucially within the key economic institutions at all levels, from small businesses to international organizations.

The toolkit that can help us conceive a better society includes the two key economic institutions that structure production and finance: the market and the corporation. They generate many of the current problems (in particular through externalities[4] and inequalities), but, well managed, they are essential to any conceivable successful society, because the market is a cornerstone of freedom and the corporation is a key collaborative institution filling the gaps of the market. The market must be handled in a way that curbs its many failures, and the corporation must be transformed into a real association of producers bringing different assets (capital, labor) together and sharing power, resources, and status in a much more horizontal way than is common in the "capitalist" economy (and including, in its governance, other stakeholders such as local communities and suppliers). Sadly, even in the allegedly most advanced societies, the worker has yet to acquire full status and full democratic rights in the "circle of respect and dignity," and the traditional form of the private company is completely anachronistic in the age of respect and democracy. Many entrepreneurs and business leaders do understand this, and the movement for "corporate liberation" is already on its way.[5] Reforming the purpose of the corporation to

---

[4] Externalities are side-effects of economic activities (such as pollution) for which market transactions do not provide appropriate incentives because those who endure the effects cannot bargain with the emitters.

[5] Many examples of businesses that have transformed their governance to unleash their employees are provided in Carney and Getz (2016).

enlarge its social function beyond the enrichment of shareholders has to happen jointly with the reform of its governance. The productive firms of various sorts (corporations, cooperatives, social enterprises, benefit corporations, sharing platforms ...) can jointly evolve and occupy different niches in the economy and the labor market, under the requirement that all of them respect the full dignity, including democratic rights, of their members, and define their social mission accordingly.

This understanding of social mechanisms and of the necessity to rely on the market and the corporation makes it possible to revisit the role of the state and to imagine a new form of welfare state that is more adapted to the globalized economy of the twenty-first century. The social-democratic welfare state is a serious option to reconsider. It is a proven formula that has shown its ability to work in open economies and foster efficient management of resources, while preserving a high degree of social solidarity. Indeed, it uses the discipline of the open market to keep productivity and profitability at a high level, it promotes efficient production by investing heavily in human capital through extensive schooling and health services, and it incentivizes the diffusion of modern technology by compressing wage inequalities between professions and between industries, forcing all businesses to be productive enough to pay good wages. At the same time, citizens benefit from the empowerment provided by education, social protection, high union coverage, and an efficient set of central institutions of social services and collective bargaining. By protecting people, not jobs, this formula combines the flexibility of the market with the economic security that households need. And the welfare system receives strong support from the electorate due to its broad coverage of the population by its universal services.

However, the social-democratic welfare state suffers from limitations which may have reduced its ability to be the leading formula for the twenty-first century. First, it requires a strongly centralized form of bargaining which does not fit well with the decentralized traditions of many countries. Second, it involves a

strong sense of responsibility and solidarity on behalf of the negoti-
ating parties, an "ethos of cooperation" at the level of society which
may also be hard to export to countries with more diverse populations.
Centralized bargaining and cooperation may also be unfamiliar to foreign transnational firms investing in the country. Third, it empowers
individual citizens to a limited extent only, because it protects them
and therefore offers them better bargaining positions, but at the local
level they do not necessarily have much voice. In systemic terms,
the social-democratic recipe is a "grand bargain" between capital and
labor but it does not really address the structural imbalance in the
capitalist economy.

A deeper form of social progress involves a more direct form of
empowerment, or, more accurately, emancipation, which involves
rights to control one's life and to participate, with due knowledge
and information, in the decisions that affect the individual's life in all
groups, associations, communities, and organizations of which one is a
member. This emancipation ideal requires a welfare state that not only
accompanies the formation of human capital and the determination of
wages, but also seeks to enforce a more equitable power balance in all
organizations at all levels.

This new type of welfare state will therefore be less about trans-
ferring resources and more about granting rights to power, status,
and knowledge in all institutions in which people are involved. This
includes the status and rights of full member in the household and
civil society associations, of full associate to the production company,
of full citizen in participatory processes in local, national, and supra-
national politics. Interestingly, this approach is already promoted in
developing countries by many actors, which shows it is not suitable
only at a very advanced stage of development, but can actually help
accelerate development, especially when the institutions are not
ripe for the complex commitment mechanism underlying the social-
democratic bargain.[6] By reorganizing decision processes to empower

---

[6] See the presentation of the philosophy of action of the Self-Employed Women
Association (India) in Chapter 5.

local stakeholders, this approach may also be able to bypass the difficulty for social democracy of getting transnational corporations involved in collective bargaining.

The stakeholder's economy that this approach envisions would contribute to driving technological innovation in a more inclusive direction, in particular in the choice of more labor-friendly technologies. If the key players of the economy were better internalizing the human impact of their behavior through their own inclusive governance, globalization and innovation would naturally have a more human face. Democratic organizations also naturally have smaller gaps between the lowest and the highest wages on their payroll, thereby reducing the need for redistribution by the state. *The more "pre-distribution" one has, the less redistribution one needs.*

This does not mean that the new welfare state – not really a "welfare" state, but rather an "emancipating" state – need not provide economic security in the form of a safety net. The market economy generates too much risk for individual earnings. It is a form of liberation, and a protection in bargaining with associates and trading partners, to be guaranteed subsistence and basic services no matter what, as shown by the social-democratic formula. But instead of distorting the economy by imposing a tax burden primarily on labor, the state can enhance the efficiency of the economy and get revenue by taxing or pricing externalities[7] and rents. This is unlikely to be sufficient, but it can substantially reduce the role of distortionary taxes. This again would contribute to orienting technological innovation in a more socially useful direction, because commodity prices (including taxes) would better reflect the social impacts of decisions about processes and products. Taxing rents can add to this efficiency-enhancing approach. Rents are revenues which reward not productive contribution but only the holding of scarce

---

[7] Since market prices do not spontaneously incentivize private decisions, an artificial price is needed, either in the form of a tax or in the form an ad-hoc market for permits.

resources or exclusive positions in a market. Reducing the net value of holding such assets via taxation would contribute to reducing the wasteful "rent-seeking" activities in which economic agents strive to secure such holdings.

This new democratic market economy is compatible with borders open to trade and capital investment, but may appear highly vulnerable to free-riding by other countries offering more advantageous deals to investors, managers, and highly skilled workers. However, the only real constraint, as far as capital flight is concerned, is guaranteeing the same level of profitability as elsewhere, and this constraint can be treated in the same way as a tax by any productive firm requesting capital investment or any bank borrowing on international markets. Even business executives accustomed to extravagant power and perks can easily get used to the new challenges and deeper joys of democratic management, just as politicians in democracies are not in scarce supply in spite of their privileges being considerably diminished compared with those of tyrants. The expansion of the democratic culture is already making the situation of old-fashioned CEOs uncomfortable in many places. Similarly, highly skilled workers can be tempted by higher wages abroad but there are real advantages to a friendly work environment and a socially cohesive society, and this will convince many to stay.

This emancipating state is compatible with decentralized institutions, unlike the social-democratic type, and does not impose political oversight over the economy. It is also quite the opposite of the socialist authoritarian approach. Instead, it infuses politics through all institutions and associations, making every citizen more involved in decisions at all levels. The same emancipating movement would have to transform standard "politics." Standard politics will remain an important sphere of society that needs some key reforms, in the current deteriorating situation of so-called "advanced democracies." This deterioration is linked with the social crisis and the growing distrust of the population. Populists accuse representative democracy of failing to give sufficient voice to those who feel left behind. The remedy is sought in more direct democracy without seeing the danger. Direct democracy tends to weaken instead of strengthening democracy, as it risks marginalizing or silencing minority views and thus may open the door to authoritarian regimes. Another worrying trend comes with the pervasiveness of the media, including social media. Politics has become a public stage, directed by attention-grabbing headlines and Twitter messages.

One can identify key elements of reforms aiming at democratizing the democracies. They have to do with political funding, media, voting rules, party formation, and the distribution of power within and between state institutions. Such reforms would in particular curb the current trend toward polarizing politics and would heavily invest in enhancing the quality of deliberation over policy. It is also important to recognize that the quality of democratic politics and the degree of social cohesion are strongly interdependent. Working toward a more inclusive society greatly advances the cause of a better functioning democracy. Political institutions are highly vulnerable to the corruption induced by social disaggregation, and the best safeguard of democratic principles is a cohesive open society with limited inequalities.

The vision defended here implies that the opposition between pro-market and pro-government ideologies is wrongheaded. One needs both a vibrant market and strong safeguards, ensured by the government and civil society, to limit the effect of market failures and empower people – just as one needs a vibrant political democracy and safeguards against the failures of democratic politics and government action. More importantly, the imagined opposition between the market and the government hides the central role of the firm, which is neither a set of markets nor a public institution, but plays a key role in the fabric of society, along other civil society institutions. The traditional private firm has historically been an important factor of economic and social progress, but it has also been the source of much social hardship and of excessive negative externalities. It can be turned into a much more positive factor of social progress.

How can this vision of a better society become a reality? A lot can be done through local initiatives. For instance, many cities have developed participatory mechanisms, many firms have horizontal and even democratic management structures, and the same can be said about shifting norms of behavior in households, NGOs, and religious communities. The enormous potential offered by the responsible and careful collection of data and their processing, which is rapidly becoming the source for firms to develop new business models and to expand their services, has hardly been tapped as yet to include citizens and not only consumers and clients. The state needs to change too if it wants to become an emancipating state, and this raises difficult issues in a globalized economy in which transnational corporations and financial markets put strong pressure on national policy. This is why the strength of the grassroots movement will be essential to trigger a real change in institutions, with the state ultimately guaranteeing for everyone the rights that many will already enjoy informally thanks to local, bottom-up initiative. The cultural shift invoked earlier is a key driver of this movement and needs to be encouraged. The UN Sustainable Development Goals are very thoughtfully structured around the notion of a "life of dignity," but remain quite vague as far as institutional reform is concerned. This book is an attempt at making this visionary set of goals a truly transformational force.

TAKE-HOME POINTS

Following the narrative of this book, as summarized in the previous section, the key messages can be formulated as follows.

1. At a peak of possibilities, we are facing an abyss: The last centuries have lifted a sizable portion of humanity out of poverty, which is remarkable, but for the coming decades, the business-as-usual scenario is catastrophic. Inequalities and environmental degradation

generate increasing physical, institutional, and moral damage and increasingly destructive political consequences and conflicts. The Anthropocene is an era when business as usual can trigger a negative chain reaction leading to the destruction of much of our collective achievements and possibly the extinction of our species. Time is running out and significant collective action needs to be undertaken very soon. Moreover, we have tremendous opportunities to improve institutions and make them work to the benefit of the population. These opportunities come both from better knowledge of what works and from better technologies making coordination and information sharing much easier and smoother than in the past.

2. We should harness globalization and technology to the benefit of all: Globalization and technological change are important drivers of current changes. In particular, they disrupt many lives, offering great opportunities to some and undermining the livelihood of others. Moreover, the economy has gone out of control because, since the 1980s, regulating institutions have been under the influence of a massive pro-market drive (more private actors, less regulation, poor supervision) and are not up to the scale of the economic action. Now many citizens are tempted by authoritarian sirens or by the demagogical promise to turn the clock back by re-erecting barriers and by spurring intercultural conflicts. Technological innovation also offers the frightening perspective of invasive technology and ubiquitous surveillance, as well as dubious efforts at commodifying or transforming humans. The key message here is that the direction and forms of globalization and technological change are shaped by institutions and policies, as well as by collectives of actors, and can be reoriented toward human needs, thereby serving rather than undermining social progress.

3. We should put the people back in the driver's seat: The traditional models of market economy and welfare state are not working well because markets fail in many ways that are left untreated, and government policies seek to protect citizens without really empowering them, keeping too many people in a situation of great dependence with respect to the labor market, their employer, and social services. Dignity is proclaimed in most countries as an equal right of citizens but many people still experience severe racial, gender, religious, and socio-economic inequalities and live in humiliation and fear. A new form of democratic market economy is worth developing, which combines universal basic protection and services, stakeholder governance in all economic organizations and especially corporations (helping them to better internalize their impacts, changing the purpose of the corporation), and comprehensive management of market failures (taxing externalities and rents rather than labor can generate revenue while enhancing efficiency). The enormous potential inherent in the new technologies, such as artificial intelligence and machine learning, agent-based simulation models, and other ways of coping with complex systems still remain to be appropriated for other purposes than increasing the profit of large corporations that are close to acquiring a monopoly over their use. Political institutions, which are now under the excessive pressure of vested interests, can similarly be reformed to better put citizens in a position of soundly deliberating policy. This fits the ongoing secular trend of increasing individual autonomy and responds to our greater understanding of collective action problems.

4. A grassroots movement is needed: The role of the nation-state remains important but we can no longer count only on the state and on national politics. Popular pressure is an important condition for the envisioned transformation, because entrenched interests are strong. Moreover, because the goal of this new democratic society is to put everyone in control of their own lives, this must logically be, in great part, a do-it-yourself revolution. Everyone can change their behavior, as a family member, as a consumer, as an investor, as a worker, as a citizen, and promote lifestyles and organizations that are more considerate of externalities and more respectful of everyone's dignity and autonomy (a large cultural shift is under way that goes in this direction). Moreover, connectedness now makes it possible to circulate knowledge and coordinate people, organizations, and communities across the world, multiplying the effectiveness of civil society actions. Education, open media, and widespread democratic deliberations will be essential to enable citizens to play a central role in transforming societies.

PART I **Sources of Worry, Reasons for Hope**

I   Global Successes and Looming Catastrophes

In many ways the three quarters of a century after 1945 have been a golden period for the world. There has of course been no global conflagration on a par with the Second World War. There has been a long-term trend of rising average income, driven by an increase in trade and technological innovation. The rising income has been accompanied by declining poverty in the world as a whole. China has registered the most spectacular income poverty reduction experience in human history. Global human development indicators such as education enrollment, infant mortality, maternal mortality, and life expectancy have improved out of all recognition compared with seven decades ago. There has been a steady expansion of democracy, with decolonization in the first half of the period and the fall of communism and many dictatorships in the second. The position of women in governance structures has improved, albeit slowly, and civil rights have advanced in many parts of the world.

But the successful global performance overall and on average hides deep pockets of slow progress and even reversal. The absolute number of poor in Africa has risen, as economic growth has not kept pace with population growth. The worst economic crisis since the 1920s hit the world in 2008, a shock from which the world economy is only just recovering. Although inequality between individuals in the world as a whole has declined because of the rapid growth of China, inequality in advanced countries like the US has increased sharply, especially over the last thirty years. This rise in inequality combines sharp increases among the very top with sharp relative declines in the middle and the bottom of the income distribution, as many traditional industries and occupations have come under pressure. These two features, the rapid growth of some poor countries and the rapid rise in inequality in rich countries, are both related to the march of globalization and technology and the way in which actors and institutions have oriented these processes. The relative gap between rich and poor countries has closed, again because of the rapid growth of countries like China, India, Vietnam, and others, but the absolute gap is large and continues to increase.

Environmental degradation and water overuse has increased, and climate change is adding further stress to ecosystems at a dramatic rate. While formal democracy has advanced and large-scale wars have receded, smaller-scale conflicts, some of them occasioned by resource stress, have increased. The rise of terrorism in the wake of these conflicts has destabilized the normally tranquil political mindset of many countries. A combination of conflict, environmental degradation, and inequalities between nations has greatly increased migration pressure from refugees looking for sheer safety and economic migrants looking for a better life. This increased pressure has in turn produced a backlash in migrant-receiving countries, especially those where middle and lower incomes have themselves been squeezed by the forces of trade and technology. In established democracies, formal political processes have brought to the fore leaders and discourses driven by xenophobia and with a strong authoritarian streak. Commentators have not been shy about making comparisons with the turbulent 1930s, when insecurity in the face of rapid change led to the rise of fascism in some countries. Even in the United States, the scenario of a proto-fascist, racist, and xenophobic government with strong sympathies for authoritarian regimes over the world, and with a volatile diplomacy dramatically increasing the risk of a nuclear conflict, no longer belongs to science fiction.

There is thus palpable turmoil and apprehension in the population as we enter the third decade of the twenty-first century, all of the achievements of the past three quarters of a century notwithstanding. The fear is that the long-run progress of humanity could be derailed in the coming decades as growing pressures on equity, sustainability, and democracy feed on each other, and the resulting tensions tear apart the economic, political, and social fabric. The successes of the last seventy-five years should not mask that we are now on the edge of a chasm. If we can successfully bridge that chasm there is a good chance that we will be able to continue on the long-run path of social progress. But it is important to peer over the abyss in order to figure out how to cross it.

GLOBAL SUCCESSES

Before looking over the abyss, let us first briefly look back at the past progress. Over the past millennium, global real GDP per capita has increased more than fifteen-fold. Figure 1.1 shows the world GDP in the years 1000, 1600, and then every four years from 1820 through 2008. The first take-off came with the Industrial Revolution in the nineteenth century, but the real acceleration came after the Second World War. The three decades after the war have been labeled "the golden age of capitalism," but for the world as a whole the six decades up to the crisis of 2008 are also a golden age. It took a thousand years for world per capita GDP to multiply by fifteen, but it took only sixty years for it to multiply by almost four between 1950 and 2008.

The numbers for individual countries play out the global pattern of success. By 1945, the United Kingdom's per capita GDP

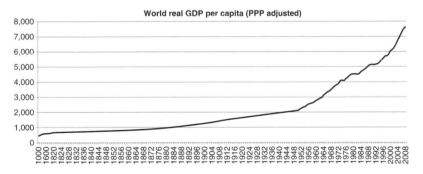

FIGURE 1.1 A Thousand Years of Global Economic Growth
Note: Purchasing power parity (PPP) adjustment tracks the real value of currencies in national markets.
Source: https://ourworldindata.org/economic growth.

was more than fifteen times its value in 1000, thanks to the Industrial Revolution in the 1800s. In only sixty years after 1945, per capita GDP more than tripled. In 1978, at the start of the reform process, China's per capita GDP was roughly twice its level in the year 1000. But thirty years later it was six times its 1978 value. At independence in 1947, India's per capita GDP was 20 percent above its value 1000 years before. During the next sixty years of independence, it increased almost fivefold.[1]

Per capita GDP is of course criticized because it is an average, hiding inequality and poverty. Unfortunately, distributional data do not go back very far, but the information we have also suggests a pattern of success at the global level over the past three decades. For the world as a whole there has been a quite spectacular decline in poverty (see Figure 1.2). The extreme-poverty headcount ratio (the percentage of population below a consumption level of $1.90 a day) has plummeted from 42 percent in 1981 to 11 percent in 2013. This sharp fall has been driven largely by the success of China, where poverty has fallen dramatically since the start of the reform process. Some have called this the most spectacular poverty performance in human history, with many hundreds of millions being lifted out of poverty in the space of three decades. Similar patterns can be seen for many Asian countries, such as India after 1991, Bangladesh in the 1990s and 2000s, and Vietnam in the 2000s. Of course, this poverty reduction is not uniform (as will be discussed next), but the decline in poverty at the global level and in many large countries undoubtedly has to be appraised as a global success of the past few decades.

The data in Figures 1.1 and 1.2 take a monetary view of well-being, and this has rightly been criticized as being too narrow. How has the world done on other indicators which capture different dimensions of human development? Figure 1.3 presents global data on four such dimensions – primary school completion, infant mortality, maternal mortality, and life expectancy.

---

[1] See IPSP (2018a, chapter 4) for a retrospective analysis of growth in the world.

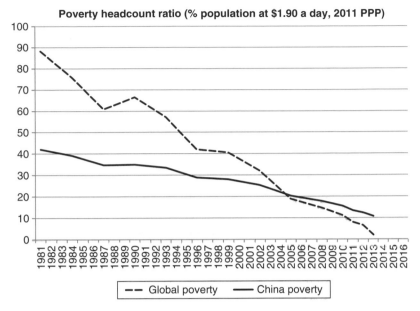

FIGURE 1.2 Three Decades of Poverty Reduction
Source: World Bank, Development Research Group.

It is clear that there has been dramatic improvement in all of these dimensions over the past half-century. Life expectancy has increased from just above fifty years in 1960 to above seventy years half a century later. This increase has been underpinned by a reduction in infant mortality from around 120 per 1,000 live births to around 30 per 1,000 live births over the same period. Estimates of maternal mortality now stand at just over 200 per 100,000 live births. This is still too high, but down from almost 400 a quarter of a century ago.[2] Finally, the trend of the primary school completion rate is also impressive globally. This rate has increased from 74 percent in 1970 to 90 percent in the second decade of the 2000s. In all of these dimensions of human development, therefore, the world can report successes on average and over the long haul.

---

[2] A detailed analysis of global public health trends is made in IPSP (2018c, chapter 18).

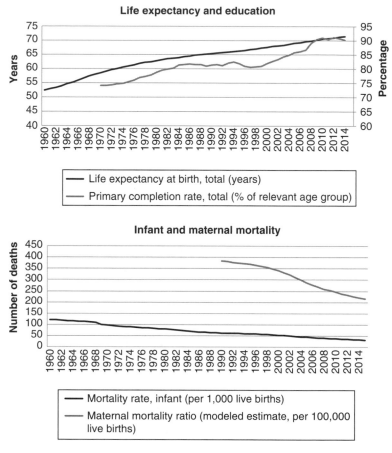

FIGURE 1.3 A Half-Century of Social Indicators
Source: World Bank database.

The non-income indicators displayed in Figure 1.3 do not capture other aspects of social progress, in particular those related to
democracy. Figure 1.4 presents some trends and patterns in this
dimension. The first indicator is, quite simply, the number of countries who are members of the United Nations. This number went
from fifty-one in 1945 to twice that number fifteen years later and
three times that number thirty years later. This reflected waves of
decolonization in the decades after the Second World War, surely a

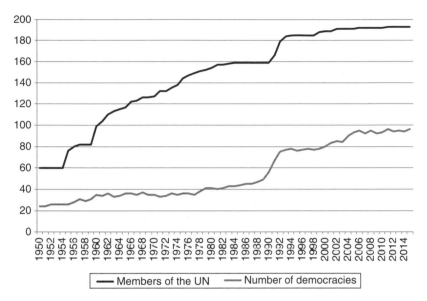

FIGURE 1.4 Decolonization and Democracy
Source: www.un.org/en/sections/member-states/growth-united-nations-membership-1945-present/index.html (UN members);
www.systemicpeace.org/inscr/p4v2015.xls (number of democracies).

shining light of global social progress through independence and self-determination for the former colonies.

But independence from former colonial powers does not necessarily mean democracy within the countries. Using the categorization employed by Polity, Figure 1.4 shows the number of democracies in the world. This shows a steady increase which matches the decolonization waves also reflected in UN membership. But a later wave comes after the fall of the Berlin Wall in 1989, when the number of democracies jumped from forty-nine to fifty-six and then sixty-seven. The numbers continued to increase as the wave spread to Africa in the 1990s. Of course, formal democracy does not necessarily mean popular participation in governing, which depends on many things, including access to information. This has been helped greatly in the last two decades by the spread of mobile telephones and the increasing social contact and coordination this has made possible. The Arab Spring is popularly said to have been helped by Facebook and Twitter. Estimates suggest that the number of people using social media globally was 1 billion in 2010, but had more than doubled within five years.

ALARMING TRENDS AND PATTERNS

Thus, overall and on average, many indicators of social progress have shown positive trends in the post-Second World War period. Why, then, is there disquiet and apprehension over what is around the corner for the world? There are other trends and patterns which are much more worrisome and motivate the work of the International Panel on Social Progress. Let us start with per capita income growth, which has shown such dramatic and positive trends as a global average. This hides poor performance in some countries alongside the spectacular performance of countries like China, India, and Vietnam. A number of countries, particularly in Africa, are mired in conflict and clearly have no growth of any sort – indeed they do not have any growth data to speak of either, statistical services being among the first casualties of state fragility.

Figure 1.5 highlights a hidden pattern which may be lost in global averages. We have already emphasized the reduction in the fraction of people below the poverty line in the world as a whole, driven spectacularly by the poverty reduction in China. Figure 1.5 shows the evolution of poverty in Sub-Saharan Africa. This shows a decline over the last twenty years – again a success story. But look at the total number of people in poverty in Africa. Although the fraction of African in poverty has fallen, the total number of poor in Africa has increased by more than 100 million in the last quarter-century because of population growth. The falling fraction in poverty may be comforting, but the rise in absolute numbers is worrying, and more-over it is a source of migration pressure and a platform for internal dissatisfaction.

If the fall in the fraction in poverty were rapid enough, it would counteract the rising population and the total number of people in

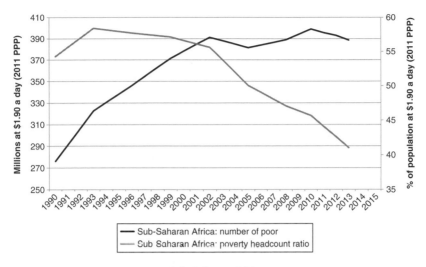

FIGURE 1.5 Poverty in Sub-Saharan Africa
Source: World Bank, Development Research Group.

poverty would fall. One reason why the fraction in poverty may not be falling rapidly enough, not just in Africa but in other places as well, is rising inequality. When inequality rises, the fruits of growth are not disseminated widely and the power of growth to reduce poverty is dented, sometimes severely. There is then a vicious cycle when poverty in turn delays the demographic transition to lower birth rates. Patterns of inequality change around the world have been quite diverse in the last three decades.[3] Latin America has seen a decline in inequality because of purposive policy interventions, although inequality is still high by world standards. Asia, on the other hand, has seen rising inequality in many countries, including China and India. One estimate is that had Asian growth occurred without rising inequality, as many as 240 million more people would have been lifted out of poverty (Asian Development Bank 2012). Finally, of

[3] A detailed presentation of the inequality trends can be found in chapter 3 of IPSP (2018a), and in particular in the longer online version (www.ipsp.org/download/chapter-3-2nd-draft-long-version). See also the important report published by Alvaredo et al. (2018).

course, inequality has risen in many rich countries, especially in the USA, where after a long period of falling inequality after the Second World War, the income share of the top 10 percent rose from around 35 percent to close to 50 percent over a quarter-century from the 1980s onwards (Piketty 2014).

The patterns of national growth and inequality change have bequeathed a striking pattern of change in the global distribution, as set out in Figure 1.6. This figure shows income growth for each position in the global income distribution in the twenty years 1988–2008. The shape of the curve captures much of the current political discourse. The gainers have been the global super-rich, and the tenth to seventieth percentiles[4] of the world's income distribution. The losers have been those in the top 75 to 95 percent of the world population. But these are precisely the middle and lower-middle income classes of the US, UK, and other rich countries. The election of Trump by the white working class of Middle America, and the propelling of the Brexit vote in the UK by those at the lower end of the income distribution are among the concrete political consequences of the famous "elephant graph" depicted in Figure 1.6.

The disconnect between fraction in poverty and total number of people in poverty shown in Figure 1.5 is caused, of course, by the high rate of population growth in Africa. The rate of growth of world population is coming down, but not world population. It now stands at 7.5 billion, and is projected to grow to 8 billion over the next decade and to 9 billion in the following two decades.[5] Growth of population over the long run is a measure of global success – the planet can now support billions more than it used to. But there is another side of the coin. Population growth and key demographic trends are the realities which the world will have to cope with in the years to come. The resource, environmental, and migration pressures of

---

[4] A percentile is the fraction of the population below the considered level. If 75 percent of the population is below your level, you are at the seventy-fifth percentile.

[5] See www.census.gov/population/international/data/idb/worldgrgraph.php; www.census.gov/population/international/data/idb/worldpopgraph.php.

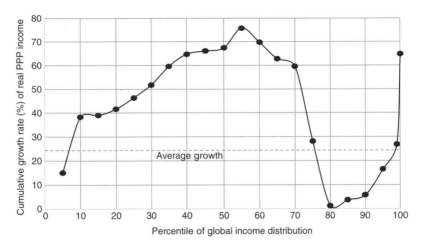

FIGURE 1.6 Global Growth Incidence Curve 1988–2008
Note: A dot on the curve represents the growth, between 1988 and
2008, of disposable income at a particular position in the distribution.
Source: Lakner and Milanovic (2015). Data available at: http://
go.worldbank.org/NWBUKI3JPo.

rising population are already being felt, particularly in certain regions
of the world. Of the 2 billion global population increase projected
over the next thirty years, Africa will account for more than a half.[6]

The age profile of the population has been changing and will
continue to change rapidly. The median age of the world population was twenty-two years in 1980 and will be thirty-five years in
2045.[7] Figure 1.7 shows that the share of population aged sixty-five
or over has been rising in the world as a whole, but particularly so
in rich countries. The rapid rise in older population in rich countries compared with poorer countries will affect the nature of the
migration pressures which are already being felt – a younger population in poor countries looking for work, and an older population in
rich countries looking to be cared for. In rich countries, it will also

[6] See https://ourworldindata.org/future-world-population-growth/
#un-population-projection-by-country-and-world-region-until-2100.
[7] See https://ourworldindata.org/age-structure-and-mortality-by-age/.

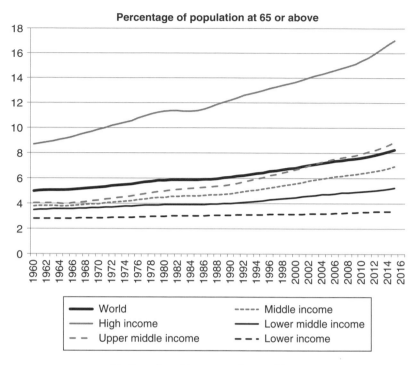

FIGURE 1.7 Six Decades of Ageing in the World
Source: World Bank database.

impact the implicit social contract as the dependency ratio of retired to working-age population rises.

The rise in world income, and the fall in income-based measures of poverty, has been much celebrated as an economic achievement and a global success. But the true economic concept of income also requires us to look at the possible depletion of assets in generating this income, and to account for it. While national economic accounts do make an attempt to measure depreciation of physical capital, standard measures of GDP do not address the state of natural capital. When such attempts are made, significant corrections appear to be needed. This is not surprising given the patterns shown in Figure 1.8. The world has been losing forest cover steadily, and water stress has increased as surface and ground water has been

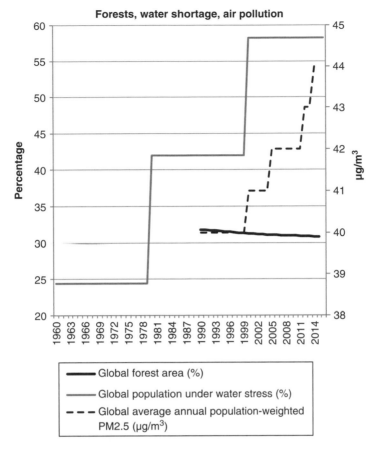

FIGURE 1.8 Environmental Degradation
Source: WDI (forest area), www.nature.com/articles/srep38495/tables/1 (water shortage), www.stateofglobalair.org/data (air pollution).

extracted for agriculture and for industry. Another natural asset is the atmosphere, which is being polluted at an alarming rate. Figure 1.8 shows a 10 percent increase in particulate matter pollution in the last quarter-century. The potential health consequences of this increased pollution stand as a major corrective to global successes on income growth.

Of course, the impact of atmospheric pollution through greenhouse gas emissions goes beyond immediate health implications.

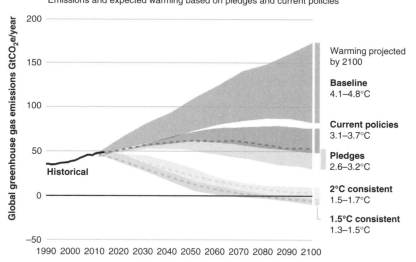

2100 WARMING PROJECTIONS
Emissions and expected warming based on pledges and current policies

FIGURE 1.9 Greenhouse Gas Emissions and Global Temperature Change
over the Century
Source: http://climateactiontracker.org/assets/publications/briefing_
papers/TempUpdate2017/CAT-2100WarmingProjections-2017.11.png.
Copyright © 2016 by Climate Analytics, Ecofys, and NewClimate
Institute.

These emissions have impacted climate patterns significantly and
will continue to do so on present trends, as shown in Figure 1.9.
The prospects for holding global temperature increase below the
critical value of 2 degrees Celsius over the next hundred years are
dismal under a business-as-usual scenario and, even after the Paris
Agreement, do not appear to be very good on the most likely trajectory. Going beyond this critical value could trigger a global spiral of
environmental disruptions threatening many species and, perhaps,
human survival itself.

Many of the global trends discussed above are leading to severe
migration pressures. Data on actual cross-border migration are
presented in Figure 1.10. The number of people with the status of
international migrants, i.e. the fraction of world population living in

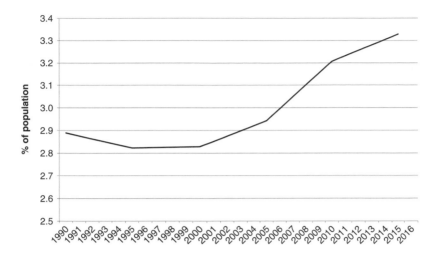

FIGURE 1.10 International Migrants (People Living Outside the Country
of Birth, in Percentage of World Population)
Source: Global Migration Data Analysis Center.

a country other than their country of birth, was just over 3.3 percent
in 2015 – around 240 million. This number was around 170 million in
2000, meaning that in the first fifteen years of the new millennium,
migrant flow was around 5 million per year.[8] On the face of it these
are relatively low numbers which belie the tensions surrounding
international migration. However:

(i) Migrants are concentrated in particular destination countries and form
a much larger proportion in major receiving countries – 15 percent in
the US, 15 percent in Germany, 17 percent in Sweden, etc.

(ii) Migrants concentrate in large cities, and data show that in many of
these cities, migrants form between 20 percent and 40 percent of the
population.

(iii) The numbers we have are official numbers on registered migrants;
illegal migration is not counted.

(iv) The numbers capture successful migration; they do not indicate the
demand for migration, which is being suppressed by border controls.

[8] Global Migration Trends Factsheet, Global Migration Data Analysis Center, 2015.

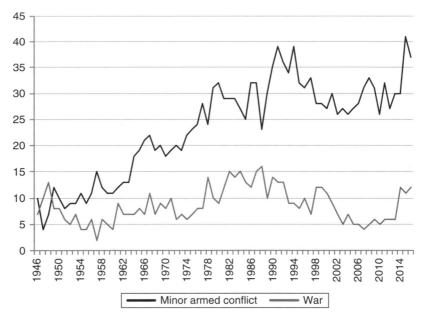

FIGURE I.II Conflicts by Intensity 1946–2016
Source: IPSP (2018b).

One result of the various tensions depicted in the previous paragraphs – rising inequality, environmental degradation, migration pressures, and so on – could be an increase in conflict and violence across the globe. Figure 1.11 presents information from the Uppsala Data Conflict Program about the number of armed conflicts. These numbers can be read in several ways. One might see in them a broad trend toward increasing conflicts since the Second World War. However, looking back from the perspective of the mid-2000s one might see a decline from the peak of the 1980s and mid-1990s. Indeed, this is the perspective that was put forward in different ways by Pinker (2011) and Goldstein (2011). However, as Wallensteen, Wieviorka et al. (IPSP 2018b, pp. 413–414) note:

> [This figure] demonstrates the difficulty of making predictions: at
> about the same time a set of new armed conflicts were
> brewing and in the following years they changed the global

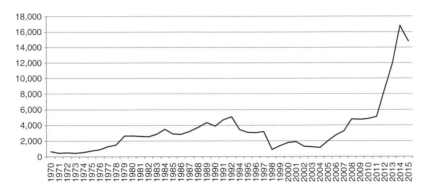

FIGURE 1.12 Terrorist Incidents Worldwide 1970–2015
Source: www.start.umd.edu/gtd/contact/.

outlook: Islamic jihadist groups made remarkable military advances resulting in large territorial gains (IS in Iraq and Syria, Boko Haram in Nigeria, other affiliates in Libya, Mali, Yemen, al-Shabaab in Somalia). The contours of a transnational coordinated movement based on military capacity and terrorist activity suggested a real challenge to the existing world order.

Indeed, Figure 1.12 shows the marked increase in the number of terrorist incidents worldwide since the early 2000s. Thus, the state of conflict in the world is another one of the major concerns to set against the global successes in the economic realm.

FEEDBACK EFFECTS AND MONSTERS AROUND THE CORNER

The previous sections have identified some of the worrying trends and patterns which should raise the alarm. One should in particular beware of the false sense of steady progress that past trends may provide. For instance, Figure 1.3 shows a steady increase in life expectancy, but hides the fact that it has declined in the former USSR after the transition, in parts of Africa during the peak of the HIV pandemics, and now in the USA for some social groups hit by labor market disruptions. The larger threats to social progress today are

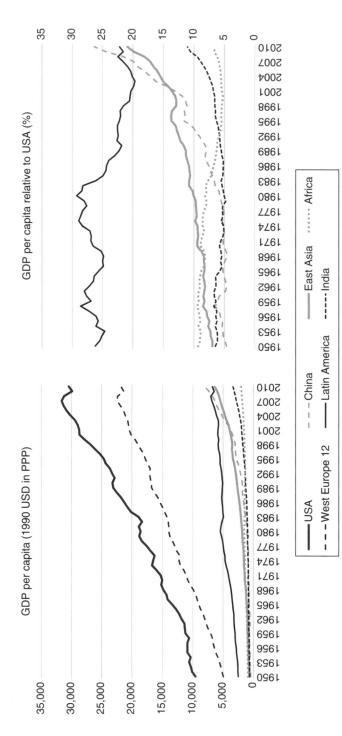

FIGURE I.I3 Absolute and Relative Gaps between Countries
Source: Maddison Project.

threats to social cohesion, environmental sustainability, peace, and democracy. As we have seen, progress on each of these fronts is now in doubt.

But particularly worrisome are the feedback effects across these dimensions which may worsen the spiral. With these feedback effects, social progress faces a looming chasm which could swallow the advances of the last three quarters of a century since the Second World War. This section discusses some of these dangerous feedback loops.

First, environmental prospects depend on development gaps and on the reactions they induce. Although, in relative terms and on average, poorer countries have been increasing their incomes faster than rich countries, the gap in absolute terms is still very high (Figure 1.13). In 2015 India's per capita income was $1,600 while that of the US was $56,000.[9] The proportionality factor of thirty-five is stark enough, but the absolute difference of more than $54,000 is equally telling. Even if India grows at 10 percent in a year, a heroic prospect, the increase in its income will be less than if the US only grows by 1 percent. The comparison in PPP dollars, with India at $5,700 and the US at $53,400, is only slightly less stark. With such inequality between rich and poor nations the demand for income growth in poor nations will continue to be high, and global climate agreements will be hostage to this inequality. But if India were to have the per capita income of the US with no change in production technology, and if this prospect is multiplied across all poor countries, carbon emissions would increase dramatically, damaging the environment considerably and threatening climate change tipping points.

The feedback effect in the other direction, from climate change to inequality between countries, is also telling. Temperature rises will enhance the growing season in latitudes far away from the equator, where most of the rich countries are located, while damaging

---

[9] http://data.worldbank.org/indicator/NY.GNP.PCAP.KD.

prospects for traditional crops in currently warmer climates as they heat up. The impact of rainfall variability or sea level rises are perhaps more evenly distributed across rich and poor coastlines and countries, but the basic fact is that the capacity to cope with sea level rises and natural disasters is also correlated with national economic wealth. Thus, even if rich and poor are hit equally with the consequences of climate change, the poor will be impoverished more, feeding into the spiral of inequality. Lack of sustainability can further feed on itself as long-established mechanisms of local cooperation break down in the face of environmental pressure on water or forests.

Environmental degradation in poor countries, the consequence of poverty and population pressure, exacerbated by climate change, can lead to severe feedback effects by intensifying migration pressure. Shortage of water is already leading to migration across contiguous borders, with rising micro-conflicts. These are adding to migration pressures and refugee flows caused by other conflicts, and such pressures are showing themselves on the doorsteps of rich countries. These are in turn leading to the rise of xenophobia and a far-right political resurgence, threatening democratic structures in rich countries. In fact, the phenomenon is also present strongly in developing countries such as South Africa and Malaysia. Here, then, we have a feedback effect from unsustainability to endangered democracy.

Rising inequality in rich countries, with the hollowing out of opportunities for the stabilizing middle class as discussed in the next chapter, is also contributing to a spiral where rising income and wealth inequality fuel politics to favor the interests of the wealthy through taxation breaks for rich individuals and corporations. Rising economic and political inequality can thus feed on itself in the current institutional structures. The long-run trends on jobless growth discussed in the next chapter are spreading globally, creating predicaments as much for the unemployed steel worker in the US Midwest as for the employees of State-Owned Enterprises in China, and creating dilemmas for African nations that cannot ride the "East

Asian model" of job-creating growth. This, combined with migration pressures, is leading to a resurgence of nationalism and protectionism, and a tendency to blame the problems of each group on "the others," be they in the country or outside. Loss of faith in the institutions of democracy is a likely consequence.

This rise of nationalism makes it even more difficult to arrive at agreements on carbon emissions and climate change, thereby worsening the prospects for sustainability. Further, as the social contract within the rich countries falters, and mechanisms for global governance weaken, the capacity of nation-states to withstand competition on environmental regulation and enforcement will also dwindle. This race to the bottom will lead us further down the spiral of environmental degradation as dirty industries relocate to countries with polities unable to resist the private and corporate incentives and willing to turn a blind eye on enforcement. These tendencies will also be present in agriculture, as manifest already in the "land grab" that is under way in Africa for agricultural land, and in the scramble for natural resources. But worsening sustainability turns the screw further, as the mechanisms outlined above are given a further twist and the spiral continues.

It is these feedback effects which should alert us to the likelihood of "monsters around the corner" even when the observed trends appear to be benign when considered in isolation. Growing polarization within and between countries, fiscal failures and collapse of states, global financial crises, environmental catastrophes including biohazards, the rise of dictatorships and banana republics, and the reaching of climate tipping points are increasingly possible in a business-as-usual scenario, even if business as usual does not look too bad along each narrowly chosen dimension in the near future.

In conclusion, the last three quarters of a century have seen by and large decent social progress, albeit with setbacks and significant pockets of no progress or even regress. But this progress should not lull us into a false sense of security. The upward trajectory of social progress of the last seven decades is now threatened by a number of fast-moving trends and patterns. These looming threats are like a chasm opening up on the pathway of social progress. The threats in the dimensions of equality, environmental sustainability, peace, and democracy are serious in their own right, but, with feedback effects on each other, they constitute a systemic challenge to social progress.

2 Globalization and Technology: Choices and Contingencies

The world faces looming crises for equality, environmental sustainability, peace, and democracy. Forces and trends – some outside our control, others the product of institutions we have ourselves fashioned – are generating deficits in all of these dimensions. The feedback loops in these deficits are such that a potential chasm has opened up on the path to social progress. This chasm explains the sense of insecurity and foreboding felt in the world today despite the many achievements of the last seventy-five years since the end of the Second World War.

Among the forces which drive the evolution of the economy, politics, and society are those of globalization and technological change. Neither is a new phenomenon. But the scale and scope of the current wave appears at least as disruptive as the previous ones. One can argue that humanity has reached a point of no return: climate change and environmental degradation put the entire planet under imminent stress and so might the likely consequences once massive environmentally linked migration sets in. It has also become obvious that the institutional responses at the global level are slow and certainly inadequate. Thus, we face the paradoxical situation that a globally interconnected world which has reached the highest level of technological development in history is lagging in its institutional capacity to adequately deal with the unprecedented challenges that confront it.

The main point of this chapter is that disruption and increasing inequalities are not the unavoidable consequences of these transformational trends, and that not only can suitable institutions alleviate the negative impacts but, in fact, the direction of the trends is itself amenable to political choices and democratic deliberation.

Globalization and technological change should not be feared or stopped, but should be tamed. Truly enough, trends and shocks beyond human control are part of the picture – only technological and political hubris would contend that we have reached a stage where everything is under our control. Nor does social progress advance in a unitary and linear fashion. But fatalism in front of globalization and technological trends must be firmly rejected.

DISRUPTIVE TRENDS

Historians have observed the occurrence of several waves of globalization in the past. Depending on geographical location, one might start with the Roman Empire which "globalized" the Mediterranean world; the discovery of the Americas which led to unprecedented transfers of plants, animals, and minerals from the "New World" to Europe as well as to a first wave of colonial exploitation; or the more recent wave of globalization toward the end of the nineteenth century which was abruptly terminated by the First World War. However, the period since the Second World War has seen significant if not dramatic increases in global connectedness in a range of dimensions, and it is this wave of globalization which is now creating both opportunities and challenges for social progress in the world.

Globalization is usually understood as the growing interconnection and integration of the global economy across national borders through trade, investment, and migration. Underpinning if not directing many of these developments is the sharp increase of global financial interdependence, which has reached unprecedented levels. The flows of goods, capital, and labor have increased in the post-war period, most dramatically in the last four decades.

Figures 2.1 and 2.2 chart the increases in the flows of goods and investment across borders. There are ups and downs, of course, sometimes severe, but the overall trend is unmistakable. For the world as a whole, trade as a share of GDP increased from around 25 percent to around 60 percent over the five decades from 1960 onwards. Foreign Direct Investment (FDI) in 1970 was just above 0.5 percent of world

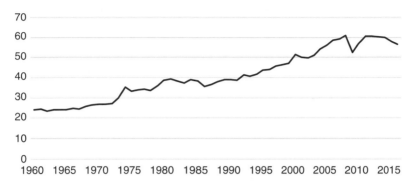

FIGURE 2.1 World Trade in Percentage of GDP
Source: World Development Indicators.

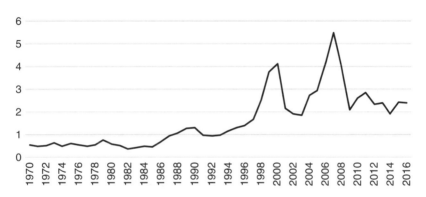

FIGURE 2.2 World Foreign Direct Investment (FDI) – Outflows in
Percentage of GDP
Note: FDI refers to investment by foreign investors setting up or
acquiring control of local business activities.
Source: UNCTAD.

GDP. It peaked at well over 5 percent just before the crash of 2008–
2009, but stood at around 2.5 percent in 2016, five times the value
four and half decades previously. This vast increase of trade and FDI
has been helped by an overall decrease in trade tariffs in the world, as
shown in Figure 2.3, and an increase in capital market openness, as
shown in Figure 2.4.

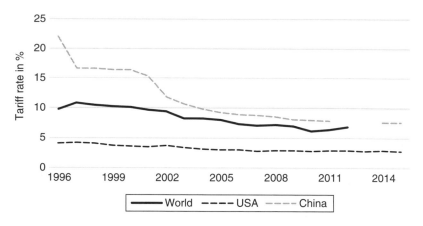

FIGURE 2.3 Tariff Rates
Source: World Development Indicators.

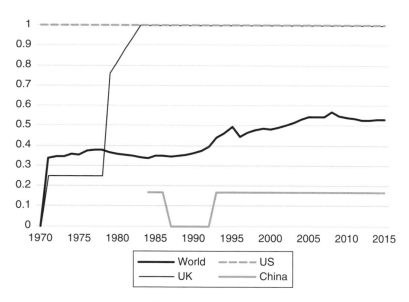

FIGURE 2.4 Capital Liberalization Index
Source: http://web.pdx.edu/~ito/Chinn-Ito_website.htm.

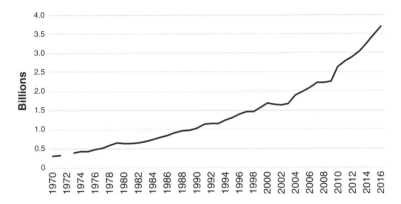

FIGURE 2.5 Worldwide Air Transport Passengers
Source: World Development Indicators.

The previous chapter has already noted that this increase in goods and capital flows has been accompanied by economic migration of people across borders – the number of people living outside their country of birth increased in the first fifteen years of this century from 170 million to 240 million. Figure 2.5 shows the sharp increase in people flows of another type – international travel. The number of air passengers multiplied fivefold between 1980 and 2015.

This growing worldwide integration has provided a spur to global growth, and a platform for the rapid growth of poor countries such as China and India. But it has produced distributional stress in rich countries, with attendant social and political consequences. It has also facilitated a race to the bottom in environmental standards at a time when ecological issues are struggling to gain wider coverage and stricter implementation.

Like globalization, technology and technological progress are subject to wave-like oscillations, giving rise to novel technological trajectories while others reach saturation or decline. They are initiated when a truly radical innovation or some major scientific-technological breakthrough occurs and eventually changes the ways in which the entire economy and society function. Technological change in the last seventy-five years has been spectacular.

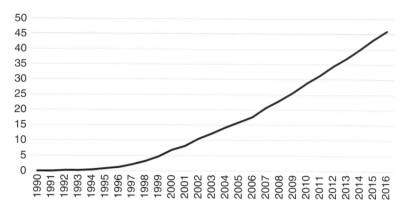

FIGURE 2.6 Internet Subscribers in Percentage of World Population
Source: World Development Indicators.

Historically, technological change in means of communication and transportation – from shipping to underwater cables, from railroads and electricity to airplanes and drones, from containers to satellites – has dramatically opened new routes while changing the nature of goods transported, as well as the mobility of people. This of course relates to the changes depicted in Figures 2.1–2.3. Most dramatically, in the last four decades, computerization and digitalization have spread into practically all sectors of economic activity and into most aspects of daily life. Over the past quarter-century, internet penetration has exploded (Figure 2.6), as has mobile phone usage (Figure 2.7). Close to half the world's population is now connected to the internet, and mobile cellular subscriptions per 100 people now exceed 100. These increases have accompanied sharp falls in the price of telecommunication.

Most obviously, new information technology has revolutionized communication and has led to new forms of work organization not envisioned only a short time ago. Automation is not only well on its way to transforming low-skills jobs, but is rapidly making inroads into professional ones. Containerization of sea freight has meant that labor-intensive dock work has almost disappeared. Strip mining and jobs for miners and financial automation and jobs for bank clerks are

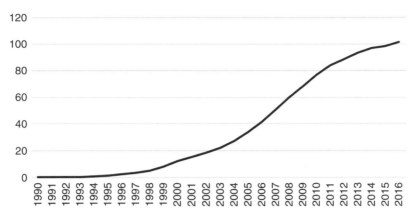

FIGURE 2.7 Mobile Cellular Subscription (Per 100 People)
Source: World Development Indicators.

further examples of the two faces of the accelerating technological march which is shaping the world around us. In one recent detailed econometric study on the US, Acemoglu and Restrepo (2017) conclude that one more robot per 1,000 workers reduces the employment-to-population ratio by about 0.18–0.34 percentage points and wages by 0.25–0.5 percent. Figure 2.8 shows that the expansion in the use of robots in the world is predicted to keep on following an exponential curve in the coming years.

One simple way of quantifying the impact of new technology on labor usage is to measure trends in the labor intensity of production, i.e. the ratio of labor to capital. The sharp decrease in labor intensity of production in the US and UK is shown in Figure 2.9. The share of labor income in GDP is more variable and has a less sharp trend, but can nevertheless be seen to be declining in the long run. These movements in market incomes have also been accompanied by changes in tax policy which have favored capital over labor, as discussed in Chapter 6 (see Figure 6.1).

The fact that these profound technological changes take place in the context of globalization makes it all the more urgent to analyze the interconnected effects they are likely to have in different parts of

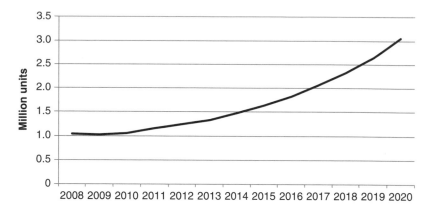

FIGURE 2.8 Estimated Worldwide Operational Stock of Industrial
Robots (with Projection for 2017–2020)
Source: IFR World Robotics 2017.

FIGURE 2.9 Labor Share in Percentage of GDP and Labor Intensity
Source: OECD stats (labor income share); www.conference-board.org/
data/economydatabase/index.cfm?id=27762 (labor intensity).

the world, as well as their unintended consequences. Technological trends have not always favored the replacement of basic labor by skilled labor and by capital. In the thirty years after the Second World War, the "East Asian miracle" was built on the advance of light manufactures using labor-intensive technology. But the tide has changed in the last three decades as technological and organizational advances have taken a labor-saving turn. Mining has become increasingly mechanized as efficient capital-intensive methods have replaced traditional jobs for miners. More importantly, it is widely expected that the automation of what were once middle-class jobs will continue. The coming wave of innovation will not target manual work, in contrast with previous waves, but will instead displace "routine" tasks, be they manual or cognitive. Even professionals such as lawyers, doctors, and professors may be threatened by the advent of algorithms, adding concerns about the "disappearance of the middle class," at least in developed economies. In the last decades it has already been observed that net job creation occurs at the two extremes of the job ladder, namely in low-paid service jobs which cannot be automatized and in high-end creative or monitoring jobs. This is illustrated in Figure 2.10 for some European countries and the USA, and Figure 2.11 analyzes the distribution of job creation over periods of expansion and recession in the USA, showing the onset of the new pattern after 1980. These and other technological replacements have had dramatic impacts on middle and lower-middle incomes, which in turn has raised inequality as well as economic and social hardship. Even in poor countries the low job creation for every unit of economic growth is causing policy concern.

Another way of stating some of these long-term trends is to look at the changing relationships between natural resources, labor, information, and capital. A report on the future security environment of the US (Ausubel et al. 2015) depicts a plausible scenario in which future use of both natural resources and labor falls, while the use of information and capital rises. The strategic elements in this scenario covering a time horizon till 2050 tend to be technological advances

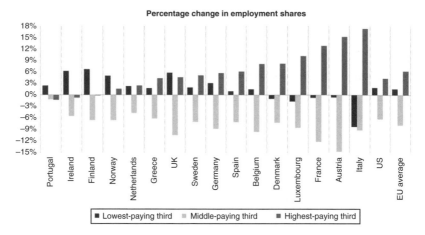

FIGURE 2.10 De-routinization of Jobs in Developed Economies
1993–2006
Source: Autor (2010); see also World Bank (2018) for a more recent
analysis in European countries.

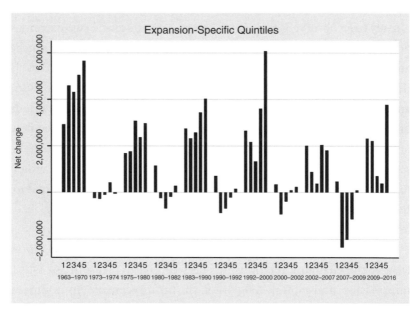

FIGURE 2.11 Job Growth across Job Wage Quintiles during Expansions
and Recessions, USA 1963–2016.
Note: Recessions use quintiles from prior expansion.
Source: Wright and Dwyer (2017).

that can be characterized as being "smaller, faster, lighter, denser, cheaper." These technologies include sensors, precision, autonomy, hydrogen, fuel cells, linear motors, rare earth elements, additive manufacturing, logistics at huge scale, sharing to boost utilization, and performance enhancement. However, such finely tuned, lean systems are also fragile and thus contain risks. The predicted shift toward the dominant role which will be assumed by information (including "artificial intelligence" and "deep learning") and capital concentrated in large corporations such as GAFA (Google, Amazon, Facebook, Apple) puts the spotlight even more on the open questions of the future of work, the use of human resources, and an overall adequate regulatory framework.

A major threat to social progress is the risk of a "digital divide." A large part of the population will be left behind if they do not have adequate access to education and opportunities to acquire the skills now in demand. In an increasingly digitalized world the *de facto* exclusion of a large number of citizens means that they also lack incentives and opportunities for political participation. Having poor or no education has significant implications for health and longevity as measured in years of life expectancy and wellbeing. Lower educational levels and a lack of scientific-technological literacy and skills also translate into a lack of genetic literacy and thus severely limit access to future state-of-the art health care. Those with little education will be excluded from the labor market, with young adult males constituting the group most at risk – not only to themselves but also to society.

Technology and globalization meet at the international level where alignments and conflicts are played out in international trade arrangements. The effect of new technologies in rich countries has been magnified by trade. The so-called "China shock" led to the equivalent of prolonged mini-recessions in those parts of the US exposed to trade with China, and affected those with lower wages and lower education most strongly (Autor et al. 2016). Despite traditional views on the efficient workings of the US labor market, these segments of the labor market did not adjust, leading to unemployment and loss of income at the middle and lower end of the income distribution.

It is clear that the mechanisms rich countries had put in place to manage temporary employment shocks have been overwhelmed by the severity and prolonged nature of the technology and trade trends. In the US, for example, Trade Adjustment Assistance (TAA) has proved wholly inadequate in terms of the level and duration of support provided. Those affected by these shocks have had to move on to disability benefits in order to get long-term income support – with the result that, under the terms of the disability benefit programs, they can no longer return to the labor market. This is another example of the potential destabilizing impact of technology and globalization in the absence of adequate policy measures to deal with them.

THE JANUS FACES OF GLOBALIZATION AND TECHNOLOGY

Social progress arises from both technological and social advances. To many it seems that technologies are the main drivers of social change. Such a view may result in a kind of technological determinism according to which people have to adapt to the changes brought about by the latest technologies. This is far from what actually happens. Newly emergent technologies usually trigger many more choices as to who will appropriate them, how they will actually be used and by whom, and which of the different possible alignments will actually shape their further trajectories. Examples range from the invention of the laser, which initially was seen as "a solution to a problem that still needs to be found," to the use of the transistor in making radios portable, and to the highly sophisticated interactions in information technology and software development with users and early adopters. The relationship between the social and the technological is therefore more appropriately conceptualized as consisting of mutually interdependent and variable processes of co-production or co-evolution. This is not to say that the social shaping of technologies should be left to the market only. Access to new technologies and the skills their use may require may have a direct impact on reinforcing existing inequalities or creating new ones, like the "digital divide" that risks driving a wedge further into an already fragmented society. While innovation has become a highly prized political goal, policy-makers often fail to consider what positive and potentially negative impacts it will have on different groups in society.

Historians of technology have argued against the largely unquestioned bias in favor of the latest technologies and innovation. They remind us that every age tends to convince itself that "this time it is different," that its latest inventions are more transformative than those that came before. Against the techno-hype of the day and an often naïve futurism they can show that many "old" technologies are still in use (Edgerton 2006). In fact, most inventions are a successful combination of old and new ideas and devices.

It is therefore important to keep these caveats in mind when approaching the task of analyzing the impact of technology on society and its effects on social progress. Multiple pathways of innovation and progress are always possible, and simultaneous inventions are the rule. Decisions over which pathway to take are socio-political choices, often embedded in contingencies, while the full range of consequences they will generate is largely not foreseeable.

One element of the diagnosis of the current malaise is thus the failure of collective mechanisms of support to adapt rapidly enough to the changing circumstances. Structures which were adequate for the post-war boom years, with technology favoring the hiring of labor and loss of employment being a temporary cyclical phenomenon, are no longer fit for purpose because the structure of employment is changing more profoundly. What follows from this diagnosis is that a more general social protection scheme is needed to maintain social progress in the decades to come. Whether society will be able to reach consensus on and develop mechanisms of this type will be a test of our collective capacity.

In particular, as discussed further in Chapter 7, redistribution of market incomes is only one possible response, and perhaps not the most effective one. Addressing the pre-distribution, creating conditions which ensure that market incomes are equitable in the first place, is a higher-order objective for the maintenance of social progress. Collective action to ensure equality in education and health are important and well discussed. However, one aspect which is far less discussed is collective action to address the technological trend directly, rather than taking it as a given to which society then has to respond through collective redistribution. The late Tony Atkinson (2015, p. 302) made the radical proposal that "the direction of techno-logical change should be an explicit concern of policy-makers, encouraging innovation in a form that increases the employability of workers, emphasizing the human dimension of service provision." The idea that technological innovation can itself be influenced by policy is not in itself controversial. It is well understood that markets may underinvest in technical progress because the benefits from it are widespread while the costs are borne by the innovator. It is also well understood that the government played a crucial role in incu-bating the internet, initially as a military technology. But what is less well accepted is that by the same token the government could indeed invest in research and development to advance socially appropriate labor-using techniques. Further, the question of technology reaches across all departments of government, not just those dealing with industry or education:

> It is not enough to say that rising inequality is due to
> technological forces outside our control. The government
> can influence the path taken. What is more, this influence is
> exercised by departments of the government that are not typically
> associated with issues of social justice. A government that is
> seeking to reduce inequality has to involve the whole cabinet of
> ministers.
>
> (Atkinson 2015, p. 119)

The same must be said about globalization. The way in which tariffs have been decreased without attention to small producers in developing countries, in which FDI has been facilitated and protected by dispute resolution mechanisms advantaging transnational firms, or in which capital account liberalization has been pursued without attention to volatile capital movements, has shaped globalization and it is possible to rewrite the rules with more socially conscious goals in mind.[1]

In June 1955 John von Neumann wrote a short article, "Can We Survive Technology?," asking some profound questions about the societal impact of the radical technical advancement in his day – the atomic bomb and nuclear energy. Von Neumann is widely known as a polymath who created the mathematical and numerical integrator and calculator at the Institute for Advanced Studies in Princeton – *de facto* the first working computer. Not surprisingly, he views technologies as being directly or indirectly constructive and beneficial. But at the same time, making a surprising connection between technology and globalization, he also sees increased instability as a consequence.

According to his argument, as technological progress advances, it expands geographically. The previous Industrial Revolution essentially consisted in making more and cheaper energy available; more and easier monitoring of human actions and reactions; and more and faster communication. Each of these developments increased the effectiveness of the other two, as well as the speed of large-scale operations – industrial, commercial, political, and migratory. But technological acceleration met its limits, as most timescales are fixed by human reaction times, habits, and other factors. Therefore, the effect of technological acceleration was to enlarge the size and to extend the geographical scope of political, organizational, economic, and cultural units. In von Neumann's view, this evolution toward

---

[1] See IPSP (2018b, chapters 11 and 12) for an analysis of how globalization has been shaped by international organizations, national policies, and international arrangements.

larger-scale operations and their spatial extension meets a natural limit – the size of the earth. This limitation induces instability, most visible at the time of his writing in the military sphere, with the two superpowers facing each other with their destructive nuclear potential.

With the benefit of hindsight, it is noteworthy that one of the pioneers of computerization and digitalization did not foresee the impact of technological evolution brought about by the wide-spread and decentralized diffusion of computers. Instead of simply performing the same operations in less time, electronic machines now perform tasks beyond human capabilities, sidestepping human physiological limitations. Communication has become instant-aneous, enabling the internet and cyber-fragmentation, automatic financial trading, satellite communication, and a host of other sim-ultaneously occurring interactions. Thus, a world has been created in which time has become compressed while spatial reach has been expanded in previously unimaginable ways.

The questions raised by John von Neumann have not lost their relevance, but today the question is rather "How to survive *with* technology in a globalized world?" Neither can we imagine a world without technology, nor is a return possible to a past of uto-pian national sovereignty that never existed, notwithstanding the manifest tendencies toward isolationism and nationalism. What has changed dramatically since the mid-fifties of the past century is the co-evolutionary expansion of unprecedented scientific-technological advances that now span the entire globe. Technology and globaliza-tion have become the Janus faces of the evolution of contemporary societies.

Yet, as von Neumann realized, technology and globaliza-tion bring not only benefits but inherent instabilities. The imme-diate doom of nuclear disaster has made a surprising comeback, with the presidents of the USA and North Korea flexing their nukes, and a worrying increase of defense spending is occurring among the major global players. Additional limitations, risks, and instabilities are surfacing. Paradoxically, technology that literally spans the entire globe and even renders a part of the universe visible from our tiny planet also heightens awareness of the finiteness of the earth we inhabit and its vulnerability to human intervention. Global issues – from climate change to the continuing migratory flows, from tight financial interconnections, carrying the risks of financial contagion, to the UN Sustainable Development Goals – vie for their place on the policy agenda. In various ways they are entangled with the technologies that shape our daily lives and interconnect us around the globe. The enormous challenges that a still-growing world population faces, such as food security, access to water, climate change, and the sustainable management of limited natural resources and assets, will hardly be manageable without the appropriate support of old and new technologies alike. Social progress on the global and the local level depends heavily on human ingenuity, political will, and the robustness of institutions to address these challenges in time. This also means the need to realize that the timescales to which complex systems operate differ from the short-termism that pervades much of our economic and political lives.

TWO TALES OF INEQUALITY

The recent rise of populism and nationalism in many Western countries, the UK referendum to leave the EU, and the turbulent aftermath surrounding the election of the US president can be viewed as a rebellion against the elites by the "losers of globalization" or those who purport to speak in their name. The "losers" are segments of the population whose subjective feeling of having been left behind is objectively confirmed by the fall in living standards, educational levels, health, and other measures as compared with the rest of the population. But even before some of these most glaring inequalities came into the spotlight, the public resonance that greeted Thomas Piketty's book was a strong sign that awareness of growing societal inequalities had reached the mainstream.

While globalization has become the target of nationalist and populist political mobilization in many countries, this has been far less the case for technologies, even if their potentially greater disruptive impact on the labor market is widely recognized. One reason for this discrepancy is that globalization has been linked to migration and the alleged outsourcing of jobs to developing countries. It has thus been easy to stir up anti-migration sentiments and to mobilize those who feel left behind to support renationalization and closure of national borders.

This anti-globalization narrative is strengthened by the recent remarkable and rapid rise of some developing countries, foremost in South-East Asia, which now boosts a growing middle class with higher educational levels and in better health. This is in sharp contrast to the phenomenon of a shrinking middle class in many rich countries. Where the middle class gives way, a growing divergence between rich and poor can be observed. Such a structural shift is often accompanied by a weakening of institutions, and a loss of trust that causes their further delegitimation. Eventually, these interlinked processes lead to polarization in society, with citizens distrusting the institutions that should protect them and guarantee social justice. The erosion of trust in institutions spills over, and eventually distrust will spread also between citizens and between various political, social, or ethnic groups. This narrative builds on globalization as the main culprit for growing inequalities, either by evoking a glorious national past or by casting "the people" as victims pushed aside by their weak and corrupt leaders or by external economic forces that privilege the rich and cosmopolitan elites.

In this account, technological change plays at most an indirect role, as it is seen to foster globalization through the increase in transportation, trade, and communications. The direct role of technology in decreasing labor intensity is not part of the story. Solutions offered in this narrative are highly simplified and mainly retrospective – what worked in the (imagined) past when national sovereignty allegedly prevailed should also work in the future – deliberately refusing to acknowledge the enormous changes that have taken place since.

Another narrative holds a significant space in the public mind, though. It also builds on the past, but in a different mode. It derives its evidence from the historical fact that the building of the welfare state in Europe was the convincing and game-changing answer to the negative impact and social misery brought about by the Industrial Revolution and the technological disruption due to mechanization. Ever since, so the argument goes, various forms of social protection involving the welfare state and the unions have demonstrated that it is possible to mitigate the undesirable effects of technological change and free trade. Therefore, taking inspiration from the social-democratic model in particular, flexible labor laws mixed with measures of social protection and security are presented as necessary today, and so is an innovation-friendly government ready to invest in basic research, but in no way blind to the necessities of regulatory (and preventive) measures of new technologies and capable of not just regulating but creating markets (Mazzucato 2013). This narrative largely blames "neoliberalism" and the deregulation wave since the 1980s for allowing social inequalities to grow. It insists that policy measures can and should correct market failures and it emphasizes the government's responsibility and capability, if only supported by political will, to "take our destiny into our hands." Globalization is acknowledged as a fact, but it is argued that it can be managed if, for instance, sufficient measures to protect existing social and environmental standards are included into global trade agreements.

In this account, technological transformations are more directly acknowledged alongside the impacts of globalization. This narrative conveys the idea that the post-Second World War welfare policies should not have been abandoned and could be revived, suitably adjusted. As we will see in Chapter 7, this narrative is somewhat severe about what happened, because many countries in Europe have kept most of their welfare policies and have been able to contain the rise of inequalities to some extent – but not the growing feeling of insecurity of the middle class and the destabilization of democratic politics. So, again, it is not clear that going back to the solutions of a previous era is sufficient to address the current challenges.

Narratives build upon and appeal to social and techno-logical imaginaries. These are individual and collective ideas and expectations about the past, present, and future. They derive their power from sharing, and from their loosely flowing, ephemeral content that nevertheless shapes expectations and, ultimately, behavior. Imaginaries accompany the introduction of new technologies, often in a utopian and dystopian version as the two sides of the same coin, projecting hopes and fears onto the immense screen of an uncertain future. To give only one example: when the internet was introduced – which was neither a planned nor a predicted innovation – it was greeted as an emancipatory technology which held the promise of being a strong equalizer. Nobody could foresee that it would become hostage to the bubbles people live in, fake news, and the celebration of hate crimes. Cyberspace has become fragmented, reinforcing the polarizing tendencies that exist in society today.

In general, in our post-communist era, imaginaries tend to be focused on technological trends and to be quite weak in their social imagination. It is easier to see the world through a technological lens, whether good or bad, than to imagine in what kind of society we want to live. It is also easy to ignore the manifold interactions between the social and technological component parts of society. Yet, the com-plexity of a social system arises from the interactions of its parts, generating newly emerging properties that cannot be predicted. The ambition of this book is to provide elements for a vision of the social future.

WHAT FOLLOWS: FROM REFLECTION TO ACTION

Our brief exploration of the twin phenomena of globalization and technology and their share in growing inequalities has yielded the following insights. First, there is a stark difference in the effects that globalization and technology have had in the rich Western countries compared with some developing countries, especially in South-East Asia, implying that responses have to be adapted to the local context.

Second, neither technology nor globalization is an external force that impinges upon societies, forcing them to yield or simply to opt out. Rather, technology is co-produced and co-evolves with society, and globalization takes many forms open to policy decisions. Historians of technology have shown repeatedly that while some economic, social, cultural, and financial conditions are more conducive to technological inventions and innovation, there is no technological determinism. Rather, initial and often contingent conditions can make a difference, leading to technological trajectories that unfold over time. Nor do ideas and innovations stop at national borders: the river does not know its source.

Third, among the larger trends that can be discerned, we note the shift in importance toward information (i.e. knowledge and technology as embodied knowledge) and capital (i.e. global financial flows, FDI, and the global interconnections of financial markets). This raises important questions about the regulation of the financial dimension of globalization and how to put it to beneficial use.

Fourth, some of the latest technological advances are strongly connected to the use of big data, algorithms, deep learning, and machine learning. While this raises many unresolved issues, including the future of work, privacy, and surveillance, again, these are not extraneous forces at work. Even algorithms are made by humans, too. These developments pose major challenges for regulating the ownership of data, privacy, and the wider consequences for security, education, work, and health, as well as how to prevent a digital divide both within countries and around the globe.

Fifth, one of the major risks and obstacles toward a more equal society is the loss of trust citizens have in their institutions, leading to polarization in society, which further delegitimizes institutions in representing and working for all citizens. This instability is at least indirectly linked to technology and globalization, as it is the well-educated and cosmopolitan elites who easily move across national borders for work, life, and pleasure, who have generated sufficient resentment to nourish a populist backlash and to prepare a distrustful citizenry for authoritarian rule. Even the idea of meritocracy has come in for criticism. With education holding the key to individual success, jobs, and income, it has been shown how the meritocratic class has devised ways of keeping others out (Reeves 2017). One must rethink inclusiveness and come up with policy measures that can mitigate the risk of further polarization.

Sixth, at the global level, it will be more important than ever to respond with consensus-building mechanisms, and the design of new institutions or reform of existing ones, e.g. the IMF and the World Bank.[2] Positive examples are the UN Sustainable Development Goals and the Paris Climate Agreement (despite their imperfections). Some of the new mechanisms could be based on shifting goals, e.g. from free trade to fair trade, or by putting greater emphasis on directed innovation, e.g. green growth.

More than ever, we are confronted with the multiple expectations people have around the globe, with their imagined futures. Historical cases reveal a great variety of choice and contingencies. The lesson is clear – it could have been otherwise. If it is human agency which determines our future, however, it is tempered and constrained by the unforeseen consequences of human action and intentions. We need to carefully consider what can be achieved or not through collective action and, especially, through having the right kinds of institutions in place. Most of our present-day institutions have been around for some time and many were designed to provide solutions for the problems of another age. We are therefore challenged to come up also with new institutional designs, adequate for the problems of today and tomorrow.

---

[2] On the key role of international organizations in the management of globalization, see IPSP (2018b, chapter 11).

3　The Expanding Circle of Respect and Dignity

When we talk about progress and its shortcomings we usually resort to concrete empirical evidence, to hard data, and to trends related to material factors, as we saw in the previous two chapters. Yet, values, ideas, and beliefs are also key elements to inform us about the world we live in and its prospects for the future. In other words, culture is as central to understanding society as are economics and technology. The very idea that society can be more just, that further social progress is possible, relies on the objective examination of existing conditions, as well as on the prevailing values about justice and ideas about improving social life. We use the term culture here "broadly, to refer not primarily to 'the arts' or so-called high-and-low culture, but to culture in the anthropological sense of the everyday social norms, ideas and identities that define the meaningfulness of social interactions of individuals and societies" (IPSP 2018c, chapter 15). Culture is what provides us with a framework to understand and give meaning to the world we live in, and what structures our anticipations about the future.

Even though inequality and injustice still plague our world, it is clear today that equality has become a widely supported social value. In other words, the idea that we all have equal worth has become something that society perceives somehow as legitimate, as positive. Controversies remain in defining what exactly one means by equality, fueling philosophical, economic, and political disputes. Yet, looking at the past, one can say without hesitation that respect for fellow human beings has been growing and that the widening recognition of the dignity of humankind signals further advances in this direction.

Many signs that humans are making advances in the art of living together can be identified in the transformations that are taking place in the way we conceive of rights, worth, and choice of lifestyles as well as in how we value diversity and alterity. To fully account for these and many other ongoing changes in our views we need to look at cultural processes from a historical perspective. We tend to think of culture as something that is so resilient that it sticks to us as some sort of birthmark. Indeed, values, beliefs, images of our world, are the cradle of long-lasting traits that characterize collectivities. However, looking at history it becomes clear that there have been big changes in the ways we humans conceive of the world. In fact, what is constitutive of culture is its original combination of change and continuity. While a short historical digression may suggest a distraction from critical contemporary issues, it is in fact a useful way to grasp the weight of culture in our lives.

What reasons do we have for being hopeful about the prospects for achieving a better society? To answer this question, it is relevant to look back, putting our contemporary challenges into historical perspective. It is useful to look at the past to understand how our image of society has changed, what the positive implications of changed worldviews are, the limits and contradictions faced, and, even more important, what can be done to make possible further progress in living together.

Let us consider, for example, that Europeans in the past conceived of themselves as belonging to rigid categories that distinguished nobles and plebeians. The common understanding was that these two social layers were substantively different and therefore there was no chance at all that their position in the social hierarchy could be changed. Sons and daughters of servants would always be servants, and those of nobles would always be nobles, regardless of what they did or did not do. Certainly, this is no longer the way we think of society. Even if the social conditions of parents do significantly affect their offspring's life perspectives, people may experience upward or downward social mobility as the consequence of their own performance and contingent circumstances. This move away from a belief in "natural" differences toward a belief in the equality of human beings is a profound cultural change, the impact of which is still unfolding.

Taking into consideration the relevance of history, here we will consider three major ongoing changes in our perceptions of the world we live in. These changes concern ideas about our interaction with nature, about the basic resources we count on to organize social life, and about the way we see the relation between equality and difference. A quick examination of such changes is relevant to illustrate the dynamic character of culture, something we often underestimate. Equally important, though, is the fact that, while touching different domains, each of the three processes affects the other two. As the following pages aim to show, together they point to the widening of the circles of solidarity and respect that tie people together, while at the same time making clear that the progresses achieved were and will be made possible by the active engagement of people. There are no blind forces of history guaranteeing a better future, and indeed human reactions and initiatives may also create obstacles to improving societal life. The choices we make pave society's future.

OUR CHANGING PERCEPTION OF NATURE

The currently growing concern with nature preservation signals an epochal change, in similar fashion to the way that the birth of the modern era was marked by a new conception of the interplay between nature and humans. One of the major tokens of modernity was the spread of the (then new) idea that instead of searching for shelter from nature's unpredictable rages it was desirable and possible to conquer nature. The faith in reason and the belief in the near absolute power of technological invention completely changed the worldview. The notion that it was possible to conquer natural forces with the resource of technology became akin to the idea of permanent material betterment as a normal process. Instead of the belief in the unpredictable turns of poverty and prosperity, with the pendulum floating one way or the other according to natural or divine caprices, a new belief became embodied in the common assumption that progress or development is the normal course of history, while economic decay or stagnation constitute anomalies, distortions that must be corrected with the virtuous use of science, technology, and policy determination.

That worldview change from a nature-governed world to a world where nature can be dominated and domesticated to serve humans lies at the core of the developmental ideology that still presides over the world. Gradually, though, we are now moving to a growing awareness that rather than conquering nature, we ought to nurture it. The concern about resource exhaustion and the search for sustainable growth lies at the core of this ongoing change in perception, the growing realization that to maintain material growth we ought to take care of the golden-egged hen.

The ongoing rise of an ecological sensibility is probably as profound a cultural change as was the belief in the possibility of continuous economic development that marked the transition to modern times. The full implications of this new way of conceiving of natural resources are still to become clearer. The idea that the continuity of development, or growth, involves not the colonization of nature but rather its preservation is quite a revolution in our way of thinking – a change of mind that is bound to have significant consequences for present and future generations. Environmental concern and nature conservation (Figure 3.1) have become for many nowadays the object of proselytism. Yet, as with any cultural change of such proportions, the mix of idealism and pragmatism is what sets the move ahead. Increasingly it becomes evident that we must act together to make our common future viable, and that intra- and intergenerational equity problems must be confronted. Although huge polluter countries go on acting as free riders refusing to share in the costs of nature preservation, awareness of human interdependence is growing in pace with the awareness of our global fate.

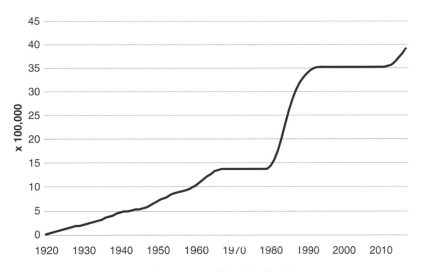

FIGURE 3.1 Protected Areas Worldwide (in km²)
Source: World Database on Protected Areas.

An interesting illustration of this cultural shift can be observed in how animals are considered. The ideological battle between animal advocates and their adversaries has been raging for centuries. Aristotle and Descartes deemed that animals had no reason and no beliefs, whereas Pythagoras and Bentham questioned the arbitrariness of discriminating between sentient species. Religious traditions also varied, with Eastern traditions (including Islam) adopting early generous stances toward animals, whereas Christian doctrines have shown great diversity up to this day – the much acclaimed *Laudato Si'* encyclical by Pope Francis does not depart on the treatment of animals from the traditional human-centric Roman Catholic approach. Although there are no long-term data on attitudes toward animals, the evolution of legislation around the world which grants animals growing protection against mistreatment is a sign of an ongoing cultural shift in favor of animal advocates. A 2015 Gallup poll shows that about a third of the US population (up from a fourth in 2008) believes that "animals deserve exactly the same rights as humans to be free from harm and exploitation," and in particular 42 percent of women endorse this statement.[1]

STATE, MARKET, AND CIVIL SOCIETY

The second of the processes of cultural change we mentioned has plenty of manifestations around the world, but its full scope and meaning is, thus far, less perceptible. It involves the inclusion of society itself as the repository of one specific resource of social organization. Until recent decades, people used to refer to state and market as the two basic types of resource societies counted on to organize themselves. We often saw countries classified according to variable combinations of state authority and market interests. Solidarity was implicitly considered as something inherent to both: to the state thanks to feelings of national belonging, and to the market via actual or virtual contracts between sellers and buyers.

This is not to say that the idea of solidarity was absent of public life in previous periods. Let us recall, for example, that the establishment of welfare systems appealed to the idea of a national solidarity. The same could be said of the ideological justification of corporatist regimes which also played with the idea of a solidary social body as the basic condition for harmonious societies. However, in both cases, solidarity was taken as the ingredient to be shaped by variable combinations of market and/or state resources. This concern about solidarity as the cement of social consensus led critics to abandon the concept of civil society which, they argued, implicitly or explicitly assumed idealist Hegelian overtones.

In recent decades, however, the resurgence of the phrase "civil society" in public discourse indicates a significant change. As the end of the twentieth century approached, more and more references appeared to solidarity as a third kind of resource for social organization. While solidarity was previously located in shared market

---

[1] See http://news.gallup.com/poll/183275/say-animals-rights-people.aspx.

interests (epitomized by labor and business unions) and in loyalty
to the nation-state, now solidarity as such starts to acquire a novel
meaning, suggesting it has distinctive characteristics. There are visible signs that the way society sees itself and conceives of its basic
forms of organization is quickly changing. New social movements
and new forms of association throughout the world point to a new
imagery: expressions such as "third sector," "non-profit sector,"
"non-governmental organizations," and "social media" gain new
currency to convey the specificity of societal solidarity vis-à-vis state
and market.

In a way, NGOs and many other forms of non-profit
organizations are no novelty (Figure 3.2). Different forms of voluntary organizations have long been among us. But the new labels to
describe them answer to the need to confer new meaning on the rep-
ertoire of resources people count on to fulfill collective needs. The
emphasis on something distinct from state and market signals the
search for alternative means to reach collective goals. The idea that
society is the repository of resources of its own introduces a new
dimension that significantly alters our perception of potentialities for
social change. It is not that society constitutes an ideal body whose
interests are naturally in harmony, but the introduction of a new
type of organizational resource in how we conceive of social life does
suggest that we can find innovative ways to solve our disputes combining three and not only two principles. It makes sense to speculate
that new forms of interest articulation and aggregation conceived
within this triple frame will add renewed meaning to politics and
contribute to reinvigorating democracy.

Developments that have been taken as indicating a crisis of
democracy, such as the decline in party membership and in adhesion
to labor unions, may indeed signal that the classic forms of political
participation have become insufficient, sometimes even inadequate,
to aggregate and articulate the multiplicity of interests at play in the
public arena. We may think of the new ways solidarity networks
have been evolving as complementary to the canonic democratic

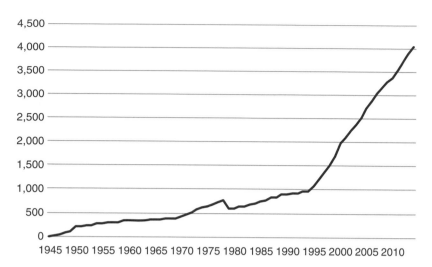

FIGURE 3.2 Number of NGOs with Consultative Status with the UN
Economic and Social Council
Source: www.staff.city.ac.uk/p.willetts/NGOS/NGO-GRPH.HTM.

forms of doing politics, more attuned to both local and transnational concerns. Naturally the various new forms of collective
mobilization we observe today need to be tested, and concerted
efforts to explore their potentialities must be evaluated before we
can decide if indeed they add to concerted efforts to institution-
alize more democratic governance mechanisms, perhaps even at a
global scale.

EQUALITY, INEQUALITY, AND DIFFERENCE

The third and last process of cultural change to be considered here
refers to the ways we conceive of equality and difference. As we know
very well, the idea of equality as a core value is one of the major
characteristics of modernity. The notion of natural differences that
in pre-modern times justified rigid social hierarchies gave way to the
idea that the opposite of equal is "unequal" – no longer "different."
To make a long story short, the very word "inequality" did not exist

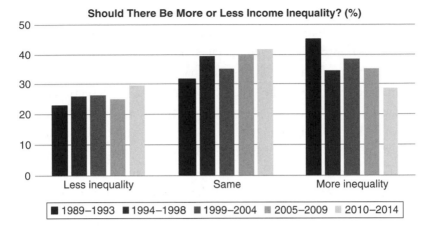

FIGURE 3.3 Attitudes toward Income Inequality Worldwide
Note: Sample – all countries (changing composition).
Source: World Values Survey.

before the idea of natural differences between nobles and plebeians came to be questioned. The revolutionary inclusion of "equality" in the banner of the French revolution marked the appearance of "inequality" as its opposite. The word "inequality" as the contrary of equality therefore has a relatively recent existence, reflecting a different way of conceiving of society.

While differences among humans did not cease to be used to justify many forms of social exclusion, their visibility was concealed under the veil of the modern concept of citizenship which made all those living within the borders of the nation-state equal. The new ideology was that as members of a common political community, they were now entitled to equal rights granted by an authority to which they owed duties and paid loyalty. Shifting attitudes toward inequalities pursue this long-term trend (Figure 3.3).

So well consolidated became the nation-state idea as the amalgamation of solidarity and authority that still today we often take it as the most natural manifestation of society: we talk about American society, Brazilian society, etc. as if social belonging was essentially determined by the borders of national states. However, in recent decades, when globalism as a shared idea and as empirical reality started challenging basic tenets of the nation-state, some of its taken-for-granted claims were replaced by new ways of looking at the world. The very emergence of solidarity as a social resource distinct from state and from market mentioned in the previous section is part of the cultural change involving our perception of society.

In fact, the notion of citizenship that emerged within the frame of the Western European nation-state model was mostly a cultural rebranding of old ingredients. States and nations were old subjects, the former referring to rulers and the latter to groups of people united by ethnicity, faith, language, or any other identity criteria. The merger of the two into the nation-state formula was a cultural product that called for identification with the nation and acceptance of the authority of the state to be experienced as a single thing. Belonging to a territory and conferring legitimacy to the state presiding over it became the head and tail of the status of citizen. The equality of individuals was the equality of citizens. Individuals shared loyalty to the nation and abode by the same laws of the state.

The fact that differences among individuals (be they gender, income, race, etc.) continued to exclude many was concealed under the success of the ideological merger of nation and state. For a long time the modern citizenship model, framed as a sort of primordial collective identity given by membership in the national community, proved able to gradually widen both the scope of rights included and the number of people entitled to them. From the Declaration of the Rights of the Man and of the Citizen issued by the French revolutionaries to the United Nations Declaration of Human Rights in 1948, a long path was trodden. There is no doubt that in many instances we still need to secure the effective rights of women and of many minorities. The criticisms that some people and organizations voiced about the Human Rights Declaration raised relevant issues. Their claims about the Western bias of the Declaration cast a shadow upon its alleged universality. Yet, despite the pertinence of such criticisms, the very pretention to universality has played a strategic role, providing arguments to confer deeper meaning on equality and to expand the scope of solidarity.

One key factor of this evolution in social norms and perceptions has been the expansion of urban life, which will continue in the coming decades, especially in developing countries. Unlike rural dwellings, and in spite of various forms of spatial segregation, cities offer many places where people from all walks of life meet and have to face their differences and inequalities. Urban space is the theater of a constant competition for space and visibility. The development of urban life has therefore contributed to the emergence of the new perception of social life as a realm of inequalities rather than just functional complementarity, but it has also made inequalities more vivid and less acceptable. Cities contain the greatest mix of social problems but are also strategic spaces for addressing such problems. It is in urban space that the interactions of diverse worlds – social, political, cultural – become part of daily life. The quest for social justice is, thus, in good part a quest for the just city (IPSP 2018a, chapter 5).

There is no doubt that progress has been made. Plural forms and conducts of life have acquired respect, many (though far from all) patriarchal impositions have been abolished, families are becoming more plural,[2] and social identities have become more fluid as they incorporate freedom of allegiance. Starting slowly in the 1960s, the differences between humans have gradually come back to the fore-front, now invoked no longer to justify rigid social hierarchies but rather to ground demands for equality, recognition, and respect. This process of cultural change has affirmed the progressive idea that equality and difference are not antagonistic but rather compatible positive values; that, together, they can provide moral justification for growing social inclusion. Secular injustices have been confronted in different contexts by specific policies aiming at suppressing deep-seated prejudices about race, gender, and sexual

---

[2] See in particular IPSP (2018c, chapter 17).

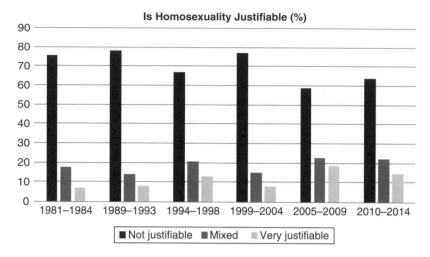

FIGURE 3.4 Attitudes about Homosexuality
Note: Sample – all countries (changing composition).
Source: World Value Survey.

orientation (Figure 3.4). We observe for example that in Brazil, where the traditionally high level of miscegenation fueled the myth of a racial democracy despite the blatant social exclusion of black people, the introduction of compensatory policies such as quotas for black students in public universities points to a significant cultural change. Moreover, collective mobilization has been crucial not only to reinforce the legitimacy of affirmative action policies but also to strengthen a black identity which in turn contributes to mobilizing anti-stigmatization strategies. Both policy initiative and collective mobilization have contributed to reinterpreting the idea of a racial democracy now as a cherished ideal to be pursued rather than a myth invoked to perpetuate inequality.[3]

With regard to gender, evidence abounds about an expanding awareness that differences must be explicitly acknowledged to promote equality. We observe for example that gender balance policies

---

[3] On affirmative action in Brazil, see Francis and Tannuri-Pianto (2013) and Telles (2004).

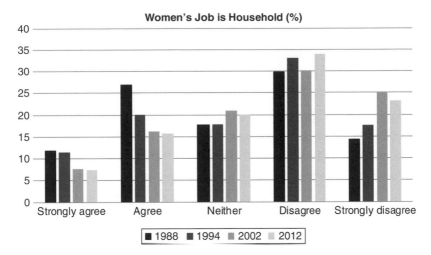

FIGURE 3.5 Attitudes toward Gender Roles
Note: Sample – Austria, Germany, Great Britain, Hungary, Ireland,
Netherlands, USA.
Source: ISSP, Family and Changing Gender Role.

are now institutionalized in many countries and significantly contribute to reducing the deficit of women in science, technology,
and politics activities perceived in the past as naturally reserved for
men. A lot of work remains to be done toward gender equality, and
women still suffer a lot not just from inequality but also from gen-
dered violence. But on that front too, things are moving (Figure 3.5).
The recent wave of protest movements on social media about sexual
harassment, which started with the Weinstein affair in the US and
has spread to many countries, echoes the progress made in the legal
repression of rape and honor killings in Asian countries or the extension of women's rights in the Middle East and North Africa.

LOOKING AT THE FUTURE

The movement to reconcile the principle of equality, as defined in
the earlier modern period, with collective rights based on shared
differences was in some sense already embedded in the notion of
equality itself. But it took the active involvement of social actors to

bring it alive. It has been the concrete mobilization of groups striving for recognition and demanding rights that made possible further advances to overcome deep-seated inequalities. Because each one of us is inserted in a particular historical context, it may seem that the cultural tradition we belong to was the one which paved the way for other traditions. This ethnocentric bias, this notion that our own cultural legacy is the reference point for humanity, is part of the myopic vision that progress has contributed to overcoming. Gradually we become more aware that the cultural changes that we commented on above are not the result of an alignment of dominated populations with "Western civilization." Quite to the contrary, various cultures in different parts of the world resist Western influence but at the same time showcase their valuable perspectives on basic human values. We observe for example that South Africans developed their own notion of social bonding and their way of handling justice, reconciliation, and reparation after severe conflicts. Among Andeans we see a notion of ecology based on a vision of humanity inhabiting the earth in a respectful way. Also in Latin America, innovative ways of involving citizens in participatory processes have been tried, suggesting that democracy can be extended beyond its traditional political realm.[4] Indians have developed various civil society organizations that coordinate and emancipate different types of informal workers. Judges in the Middle East and North Africa have granted greater rights to women in matrimonial affairs from within the general Islamic framework. In conclusion, far from embracing Western values, one sees that the world converges, perhaps, by a slow selection of the values that generate the least suffering and the least resistance.

In a globalized world, contacts among cultures offer opportunities and risks of enriching or impoverishing cross-influences. It is not too difficult, in the post-colonial world, to see that the most promising approach is that of a respectful dialogue across cultures (e.g. about how to view the place of human life in the cosmos, the place

---

[4] More on this in Chapter 8, and in IPSP (2018c, chapter 14).

of the individual in the group), with the possibility of mutual evolution. Corroborating our observation that equality and difference, previously perceived as antagonistic, are increasingly perceived as instrumental to each other, the Western idea of modernity viewed through the lens of individualization and separation from traditional bonds is actually receding given the imperious human need for social inclusion.

Looking at the historical development of the equality ideal and its concealment of differences, it becomes clearer why the need for recognition has emerged in the last decades as crucial among groups that were or still are deprived of access to full membership in their social contexts. Recognition has become a key element in claims for equality that mobilize gender, ethnicity, religion, language, or any other possible specificity that implicitly or explicitly has been used to deprive groups of people of the equality that traditionally grounded notions of membership in national communities. Furthermore, increasingly we observe demands for the recognition of identities posed by groups that do not see their particularity as being in conflict with national identity. Many who now claim for the recognition of their group distinctiveness see it as a condition for the affirmation of their individuality. The view that identities are chosen and contingent is registering growing acceptance, not as the negation but rather as the full affirmation of individuality.

The way our conceptions of difference, equality, and inequality have evolved provides a good illustration of the dynamics of culture. The equality ideal has had a definitive impact in expanding the circle of human solidarity, but it is not something that automatically envelops society. Its developments are tied to the active involvement of individuals and groups which, striving to reach concrete goals, add more meaning to equality. These are the dynamics of the cultural shift toward the "cosmopolitization" of societies, the pluralization of families, the acceptance of racial, gender, and religious diversity – processes that seem to be irreversible.

To the extent that human actions set the world in motion, regress is also possible. We know that backlash and resistance can be strong and violent. We continue to be confronted with many situations that openly contest the observed progressive trends. However, it is crucial to have in mind that, rather than constituting manifestations of a clash of civilizations as some pretend, such violent reactions point to desperate attempts by specific groups to counteract the potential for tolerance and understanding. We have good reasons to hope for a situation where common values can be shared while differences are respected. A shared respect for diversity can constitute the cement of a generalized feeling of respect among people. Incorporating the value of diversity, we enable ourselves to fight for a more egalitarian, more tolerant, and more enriched world. Yet, it is not in the comfort of relativism that we pursue tolerance. Social justice, human rights, fraternity remain universal values, the ethical ground that justifies the active engagement of responsible social actors.

In addition to the fallacious argument about an irremediable clash of worldviews, we must also caution ourselves against the opposite view that foresees an irremediable convergence of cultures. The idea that the ongoing process of globalization will extinguish traditional cultures, reducing the world to single pattern of customs, practices, and ideas, constitutes another fallacy. To sustain it one must ignore that culture is precisely this unique combination of change and continuity. History shows us that humans change their worldviews while at the same time keeping their distinctiveness thanks to long-established traits peculiar to their background.

Because we all are inevitably immersed in historical processes, what we inherit from the past is reprocessed in the present but somehow remains alive. From this is derived the fact that while common ways of acting and thinking become shared on a global scale, local cultures remain alive and may even gain strength to the extent that improved resources of communication and greater visibility also contribute to renewed solidarity. It has been observed that people who emigrate are often the ones who take the lead in using social media as an instrument to reconnect with their cultural origins and, in the effort to forge an identity in the new context, contribute to reviving traditions. It has been reported for example that in some African countries fading religious and lay celebrations gained renewed strength in recent years while helping to bring together residents and non-residents. Also illustrative are reports about geographically segregated native communities that find support for their claims to preserve their traditions in the wider social networks around the globe. Lower levels of governments such as regional states, provinces, or cities have in some cases offered the relevant scale for introducing experimental social reforms and community initiatives, becoming strong vectors for social progress at a larger scale.

The examples mentioned above suggest that the apparent contradiction between two distinct types of culture, one global and one restricted to smaller groups, has rather been a positive element in expanding the human circle of solidarity. As people realize the possibility of sharing values without renouncing their singular ways of being and acting, they build solid bridges that enhance mutual understanding, signaling that we may belong to a larger solidarity circle without giving up ways of living shared only with restricted groups.

All things considered, the realization that our conception of society has been historically changing to dislodge deep-seated prejudices spells promising perspectives for the future of humankind. Reflecting about the big cultural transformations that have taken place during the last 200 years or so, we indeed observe that the circle of respect and dignity has grown. Furthermore, the call for the social inclusion of the many still left behind remains alive, as eloquently stated in the United Nations' Sustainable Development Goals. The notion that what makes us fellow humans is the fact that we share an equal worth has made progress. The idea that we are equal to the extent that we share our very humanity remains a driving cultural force.

However, as already mentioned, we must constantly recall that even though we can identify a long-term cultural process of overcoming deep-seated views about allegedly natural human differences justifying inequality, we should not deduce from this that history merely fulfills a manifest destiny toward progressive social equality and expanded solidarity. The concrete actions of people are the forces that set in motion changes in the ways we look at the world. That is why cultural elements can contribute to forging progress as well as unleashing retrograde forces.

No automatic social progress is assured. As observed in previous chapters, inequality is rampant within and between countries. There is plenty of evidence that the move toward expanded solidarity meets strong reactions in many contexts and faces setbacks that may even put into danger progress already achieved. Let us recall, for example, that ethnic and religious minorities have been persecuted in several contexts, or that women's claims for rights have been met with violent responses in more than one country. Examples abound of the systematic discrimination and even open persecution that the world still lives with. Sad illustrations here are the victimization of Christians in contemporary Nigeria, or the atrocious legal and illegal punishment of homosexuals that still occurs in many countries. According to recent reports, homosexuality is punishable by death in Sudan, Iran, Saudi Arabia, and Yemen, and in parts of Nigeria and Somalia. Statistics on violence against women show that it goes on throughout the world, and let us recall the dramatic accounts of Pakistani and Afghan girls who are victims of violence just because they dare to enroll in schools.

There are even retrograde attempts to curtail already-established human rights in affluent and long-established democracies, as dramatically illustrated by ongoing developments curtailing freedom within what we used to consider mature democracies.

Be that as it may, the progress achieved in social life constitutes both cause and consequence of cultural changes that emerged not as blind forces but as the result of human efforts. Striving to secure specific ideals and interests, people get together, often contributing to advancing goals in ways they did not anticipate, and thus becoming part of long-run moves toward expanded solidarity. It was a long process of mobilization for specific causes that converted the values of equality and universal human worth into common cultural currency. That is why contemporary violators of these values must recur to excuses, disguises, and apologies. It is no longer socially acceptable to sustain the view that some sorts of people naturally have worth while others are naturally devoid of it. We rarely meet people arguing for the desirability of preserving inequality as such. The rhetoric of those who stand against measures to reduce income inequality, for example, usually contends that such measures will backfire, implicitly condoning the ethical value of equality.

While each of the three big cultural changes we have mentioned have had specific consequences, they are part and parcel of a global change, the most general feature of which is a growing awareness of the common fate of humans. This awareness underlies the claims for global environmental protection, for enlarging the circle of solidarity beyond national borders, and for conceiving of people's differences as deserving respect within the converging planetary fate we all share.

The amazing jigsaw of cultures, with their mix of continuity and change, is part of the human adventure. To persist as well as to change, ways of conceiving of the world depend on the active involvement of real people. The ideas of respect for differences are engaged with, and demands for equality and for recognition are enforced, not as the defense of abstract principles, but as the principled defense of concrete causes. But whatever these causes are, education and access to culture must be supported to help create (or consolidate) the atmosphere of tolerance and mutual recognition among individuals. Learning about others and sharing in their experiences are powerful instruments in deconstructing the symbolic borders that convert differences (be they religious, ethnic, national, or racial) into barriers to mutual understanding. Awareness of the richness of human diversity has been slowly growing, in large part thanks to the active involvement of educators and cultural entrepreneurs.

As IPSP (2018c, chapter 19) discusses at length, education, and increasingly higher education as education levels rise for a fast-growing part of the population around the globe, can be a powerful instrument to promote progress, not just because it contributes to forming human capital in the strict economic sense but also because it works to widen one's perception of the world and its possibilities. As one learns about other ways of living, other views of the universe, new windows actually become new doors to the future. In this way, though multiple modernities are emerging in various parts of the world, they may all suggest, with many variants, an ideal of a balanced combination of the individual and the whole in everyone's perspective of what makes life valuable. In this ideal, the collective life is part of the individual life, as something that gives meaning and goals, and colors basic values such as liberty, equality, and harmony with nature.

4   The Big Challenge

The previous chapters have shown that very serious threats are hovering over the world, primarily caused by human action, bad institutions, and bad policies. But these chapters have also offered reasons for hope. Globalization and technology are not enemies of the human species; they can be tamed and reoriented to serve populations better. And attitudes toward races, genders, sexual orientation, animals, and nature are slowly changing toward greater respect. This cultural trend is a great asset in fostering better social relations and better environmental management.

This chapter lays the task ahead in a more precise way, and gives a warning: It will not be easy. We cannot simply undertake minor changes, small fine-tuning of policies, and avert the looming crises. A more fundamental transformation is needed. We believe that this transformation is possible, and in the second part of the book we will explain how it can be envisioned. For the time being, let us examine the challenging task that the world is facing.

The task ahead can be summarized in this way. Three main goals must be pursued and achieved in conjunction, and they relate to three fundamental values:

- Equity: reduce inequalities of development between countries and social inequalities within countries;
- Sustainability: put the planet back on a track that preserves ecosystems and the human beings of future generations;
- Freedom: expand and deepen basic liberties, the rule of law, and democratic rights for all populations.

These three goals appear prominently in the UN Sustainable Development Goals of the Agenda 2030, among many other goals (there are seventeen in total). However, the other goals can be tied to these three, which serve as useful flag-bearers of the main issues that need to be tackled by the world in this century.

What is challenging about these three goals is that each of them is necessary for the development of a positive scenario for social justice and the future of the planet, but their combination is not obvious because seeking to pursue two of them induces a potential tension with the third one. Scenarios in which two are successfully realized at the expense of the third are useful benchmarks against which to analyze the pitfalls awaiting us in the future, the ways in which we might *fail* to avert the looming catastrophes described in Chapter 1. This chapter, then, explores the three "failure" scenarios where one goal is missed. The purpose is not to convey a "doom and gloom" perspective, but to help identify the relevant challenges, and better explain why none of the goals can be sidelined and neglected. These scenarios also show why achieving two of the goals may appear easier if the third one is dropped. The second part of the book will explore how to pursue the three goals simultaneously.

THE APARTHEID SCENARIO

Imagine the world in 2050, in a scenario in which significant achievements can be celebrated on the fronts of freedom and sustainability, but not on the front of equity. In this scenario, the share of the population living in democracies has continued to increase, as could be hoped from Figure 1.4. The increase has occurred mostly thanks to the political opening of China around 2030, in which an educated and affluent population could no longer be governed in the old way.

Regarding sustainability, after some hesitation the USA and China, later joined by India, have gathered with Europe to promote research and investment in renewable energy and reduce the emission of greenhouse gases drastically. The apparent slowdown at the end of the curve that one could examine when this book was written, as shown in Figure 4.1, has turned out, after a last bump in 2017–2019,

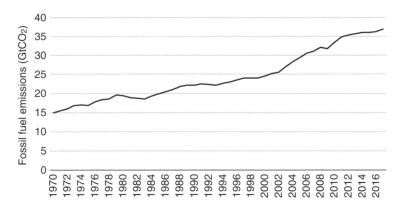

FIGURE 4.1 Emissions of CO₂ Worldwide
Source: Global Carbon Project and T.A. Boden, G. Marland, R.J. Andres 2017, *Global, Regional, and National Fossil-Fuel CO₂ Emissions*, Oak Ridge National Laboratory, Oak Ridge, Tenn., http://cdiac.ess-dive.lbl.gov/trends/emis/overview_2014.html.

to mark the peak of world industrial emissions of CO_2 and the real start of the green transition for the developed world.

Thanks to this momentum led by the main emitters, and the absence of new emerging economies, the concentration of greenhouse gases in the atmosphere seems on good tracks to keep average temperature below an increase of 2°C above the pre-industrial level at least until the end of the century. The picture in relation to other issues such as biodiversity and water management is less rosy, especially because the lack of development in many parts of the world, particularly at low latitudes, leads to failures in the preservation of wildlife and poor water infrastructures. Conflicts over water use in the Middle East and Sub-Saharan Africa jeopardize political stability there.

The key problem with this scenario, indeed, is that the equity goal has been missed. In fact, development has continued pretty much along the path initiated in the beginning of the century. Some promising signs had then seemed to appear when the distribution of income, worldwide, moved from a polarized pattern, in which the rich countries had distanced themselves from the rest of the world and created a separate vanguard "heap" in the shape of the distribution, to a single-heap pattern showing some catching up (see Figure 4.2, which stacks the income distributions of the various regions of the world to form the world distribution).

But this promising movement was almost entirely due to China crawling upward along the top of the heap and forming a big central bulge with its large population. If one removed China from the graphs, the improvement would seem much more modest, and the two separate heaps would remain distinct. By the middle of the century, continuing along similar trends, China has caught up with Europe and the USA, and India has started a significant catch-up move. Latin America has grown at a pace that is not sufficient to reduce the gap with the rich countries. Indeed, a growth rate of 1.5 percent added more than $450 to the average income of an American in 2010, whereas Latin America would have needed a growth rate of 6.6 percent to simply keep the distance. The real drama is Africa, which, in 2050, has failed to take off, after false starts by a few countries such as Ethiopia, Ghana, and Malawi, due to overwhelming political problems fueled by ethnic and religious violence as well as ecological disasters.

Figure 4.3 projects economic growth in the various regions of the world, assuming that they have, since 2010, kept up the 1990–2010 growth rates (for China, the growth rate is 6 percent, lower than the average 7.6 percent observed over 1990–2010, but nevertheless sufficient to catch up to rich countries).

By 2050, the difference in living standards between the rich and the poor has become so breathtaking that it is impossible for migratory pressure not to rise to gigantic proportions. Moreover, population in Africa, following projections made earlier in the century, has more than doubled, having increased by 1.3 billion people between 2015 and 2050. The sad aspect of this scenario is that the rich countries, in spite of their declining and ageing populations, and actually because of this demographic pattern – which made their electorate

(a)

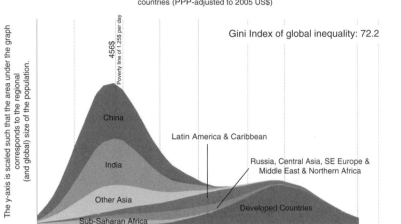

(b)

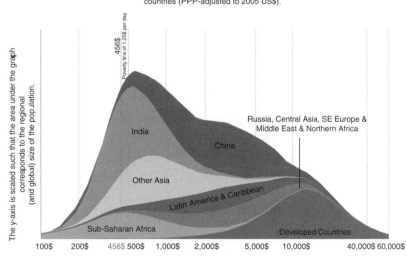

FIGURE 4.2 Distribution of Income Worldwide
Source: Our World in Data.

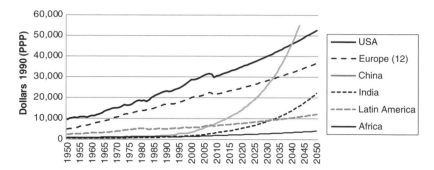

FIGURE 4.3 GDP Per Capita in the World (1950–2010; Projection to 2050)
Source: Maddison Project for 1950–2010; own calculations for projections.

radicalized supporters of their national identity and afraid of cultural diversity – have kept the doors shut to the needy masses of the poor countries. The situation of "global Apartheid," in 2050, appears completely untenable and the staggering costs of walls and border patrols, the shocking numbers of migrants who die trying to cross electric fences and dangerous waters, foretell a major crisis in the coming years.

It is of course hard to imagine a massive migration without a serious disruption of receiving as well as sending communities. The migration issue has been politically volatile in Europe and the USA since the end of the twentieth century, even though the numbers of the migration flows have been ridiculously small compared with the scale of the potential migrations. In 2050, there is much more reason to worry about the likelihood of violent, large-scale ethnic conflicts in Europe and the USA, even civil wars, in case of massive influx.

Migrations are not the only source of stress. Huge gaps in living standards feed a strong resentment in former colonies left behind, fostering disputes in global institutions (as witnessed in the fall of the global institutions created in the twentieth century), as well as local violence and global terrorism.

Another related and worrisome feature of this scenario is that inequalities within countries have also continued to increase. In particular, the top 1 percent and even more the top 0.1 percent have continued to reap greater shares of income and have amassed considerable wealth. The connection between international and national inequalities is the fact that identity politics and even populist rhetoric have been used to quell social protests. Starting in Europe with the Brexit vote and in the USA with a rocky Trump presidency, multilateral trade agreements have unraveled and foreign aid has dwindled. Globalization has been abruptly curbed and this has undermined the possibilities for the poor countries to take off.

Meanwhile, the national inequality trend has continued almost unabated. A form of internal Apartheid has emerged, in which the wealthy do not confine the rest of the population, but instead retreat themselves into exclusive, private domains and adopt a way of life that does not rely on goods and services provided by the state, even for the protection of private property, which is handled by security companies.

The "left behind" of the world, in this scenario, do not unite. On the contrary, the only glue that keeps the working classes of the rich countries tied to politicians that do not serve them well is the promise to keep the doors shut to the competition of migrants and to crack down on minorities. Political and religious extremists or terrorists gain importance as their violent acts offer highly mediatized ways to contest the unsatisfactory state of affairs locally and globally. Nationalistic and racist rhetoric assuages social unrest. The wealthy elite does not buy into the closed-border or racialist mystics, but is willing to tolerate this as the only way to preserve its privileges. In such a situation, the liberal cosmopolitan intellectuals are in disarray because their pleas for more generous policies within the developed countries and toward the less-developed countries fall on deaf ears – most of the population does not want to hear about at least one part (the internal or the external) of this generosity package.

Let us end this dystopic scenario here. There is no future without equity. In the celebrated 1987 report *Our Common Future*, prepared under the leadership of the former Norwegian prime minister Gro Harlem Brundtland, sustainability is defined as relying on three pillars: the economic, the social, and the environmental. Equity, the reduction of inequalities, is essential for the social pillar. In this scenario, one even sees that the progress of freedom and democracy can only be very limited, and is seriously jeopardized by populist excesses in national politics.

The challenging aspect of this scenario is that leaving an important part of the world population in a state of under-development is part of the equation that makes it a success for sustainability, at least for the climate problem. The question to be addressed later in this book is, then: What needs to be changed in this scenario in order to combine equity with sustainability, in a free world?

THE "END-OF-HISTORY" SCENARIO

Here is another scenario that espouses Francis Fukuyama's view that the institutions of the "free world" represent the ultimate stage of humanity. In this view, the market economy and the political institutions of liberal democracy are the key to economic and human development, and nothing better has been invented.

Imagine, then, that the elites that meet in Davos have finally recognized that the world cries out for a better management of social cohesion, both at the international and at the national level. They have understood that growing inequalities will ultimately make migratory movements run out of control and feed increasingly disruptive protest movements. They have been worried about Podemos and Syriza, but they have been even more frightened by Orban, Erdogan, Putin, and Trump, because while left-wing populism brings business-unfriendly economic and social policies, right-wing populism brings back the prospect of war. And they have also recognized that the high degree of corruption that plagues most countries, both in economic investments and in the political game show, has to be drastically curbed if one wants to restore the public's trust in institutions.

One should not imagine that economic and political elites are always greedy and myopic. Consider for instance what happened when Ronald Reagan tried to slash the Environmental Protection Agency (EPA) in 1980, rolling back regulations that he viewed as hampering business development. Within two years, the public had lost confidence in both government and business for the preservation of a healthy environment (especially in water and air), and the EPA was the epicenter of many fights. Reagan called upon Michael Ruckelshaus,[1] who had been in charge of the EPA under Richard Nixon, to come back to Washington to fix the situation. To Ruckelshaus' great surprise, the chemical industry rushed to meet him and pleaded that strong environmental regulation and a robust EPA were needed to restore the public's trust in the industry. When things become really bad, the elites ultimately see that their long-term interest involves making concessions to the demands and needs of the population.

So, in this scenario, the efforts at cleaning up institutions in most countries have strengthened the rule of law, improved stability for investors, and enabled many countries to take off and start their catch-up path toward decent living standards for most of their populations. Similarly, in developed countries, freeing the political institutions from capture by economic and financial interests has enabled the population's strong desire for more equitable social policies and greater redistribution to be listened to and eventually implemented, including in countries such as the USA and the UK where strong conservative movements had tried to undermine social policies except those that served pensioners. In the World Values Survey, one sees that in the beginning of the twenty-first century, the support for greater equality of income and for democracy is growing

---

[1] www.nytimes.com/2017/03/07/opinion/a-lesson-trump-and-the-epa-should-heed
.html?ref=opinion&_r=0.

Table 4.1 *Support for Equality and Democracy*

Countries	Support for equality*		Support for democracy**	
	2005–2009	2010–2014	2005–2009	2010–2014
Australia	45%	61%	91%	88%
Chile	60%	76%	82%	90%
China	34%	62%	79%	85%
Egypt	32%	64%	97%	97%
Germany	65%	75%	96%	92%
Russia	39%	74%	69%	72%
Sweden	36%	59%	99%	96%
United States	37%	48%	85%	84%

Notes: *Percentage of respondents considering that they endorse the statement "incomes should be made more equal" more than the statement "we need larger income differences as incentives for individual effort."
**Percentage of respondents leaning more on the side of "it is absolutely important to live in a country that is governed democratically" than on the side of "it is not at all important."
Source: World Values Survey, www.worldvaluessurvey.org/WVSOnline.jsp.

for the former and very strong for the latter, as illustrated for a few countries in Table 4.1.

This scenario therefore manages to combine an expansion of the rule of law, freedom, and democracy on the one hand, and a reduction of income inequalities and a convergence of living standards on the other hand. The dream of a combination of well-regulated market economy and clean liberal democracy is indeed able to deliver good outcomes on these two fronts, even if, as we will argue in the second part of this book, social justice requires more than just curbing income inequalities.

The problem with this scenario is that the spread of the "end-of-history," i.e. Western, institutions is accompanied by a spread of the Western way of life, and this is catastrophic for the planet. Van Benthem (2015), echoed by a recent report by the World Bank

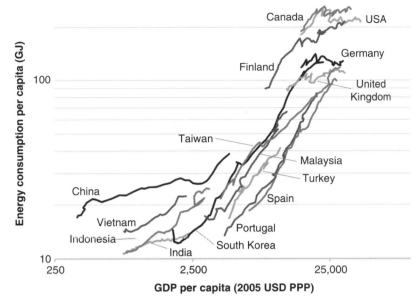

FIGURE 4.4 Energy Consumption at Different Levels of Development
Source: Benthem (2015, fig. 1).

(Hallegatte et al. 2016), points out that scenarios for energy consumption that assume "leap-frogging" by developing countries, i.e. the widespread adoption of new technologies that are more energy-efficient, do not appear realistic. As Figures 4.4 and 4.5, drawn from van Benthem's work, show, the developing economies do not improve on the path followed by the developed economies, and may even appear to do worse, in the sense that at the same level of GDP per capita, they consume more energy per capita.

Figure 4.5 performs a similar comparison to Figure 4.4, at two dates: the industrialized countries in 1960 (gray boxes) and the less-developed countries in recent years (black boxes). The explanation for these sobering facts appears to lie in the adoption of higher-energy forms of consumption in the emerging economies, such as greater use of automobiles, for a given level of development. One can perhaps interpret this as reflecting the desire of newly affluent people to adopt visible and energy-expensive symbols of an iconic consumerist lifestyle.

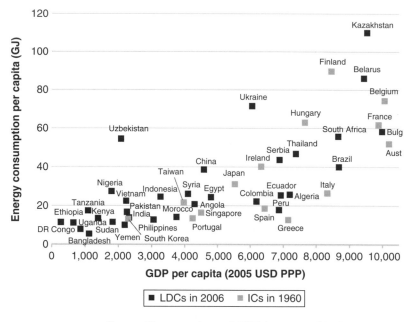

FIGURE 4.5 Energy Consumption and GDP in 1960 and in Recent Years
Notes: LDCs = less-developed countries; ICs = industrialized countries.
Source: Benthem (2015, fig. 2).

Energy consumption is only one token of a more general devastation that destroys ecosystems, accelerates the sixth mass extinction of species that is ongoing, disrupts the climate, and prepares a very difficult world for future generations.

For instance, the fact that, in this scenario, one after the other, the populations of the world take the conveyor belt of economic development, reproduces the acceleration of CO_2 emissions observed in Figure 4.1 for the first decade of the century. As shown in Figure 4.6, this acceleration was entirely due to the growth of emerging economies, that is, mostly China.

In conclusion, this scenario is the dream scenario that one could have imagined in 1970, before the awareness of climate and environmental threats dawned on us. Economic and human development spreads alongside the expansion of freedom and democracy throughout the world. This scenario would be a very positive scenario

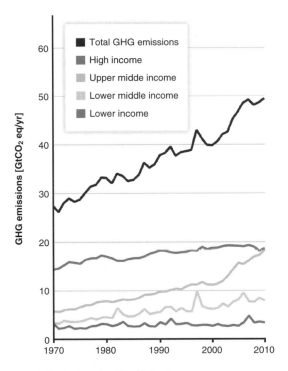

FIGURE 4.6 Emissions by World Regions
Source: IPCC AR5 Technical Summary, fig. TS4.

if the human population was not so large and careless on such a small and resource-limited planet. Unfortunately, the old-fashioned form of development is bound to hit a wall. As the joke goes, if you believe in continued exponential growth, you are either a mad person or an economist.

Sustainability can be defined as the compatibility between current actions and the preservation of future generations' chances to be at least as well off; more stringent variants of this notion that do not only focus on human wellbeing but also include the preservation of ecosystems can also be usefully considered.[2] To be honest, we already know that our life on earth will not be possible in about

---

[2] On sustainability and its measurement, see IPSP (2018a, chapter 4).

500 million years due to excessive radiation from the Sun, and experts consider it actually unlikely that our species will still be around in 2 million years. At some point, even assuming interstellar travel, things will turn badly for our descendants. The question is therefore not whether our current wellbeing is sustainable forever – it is not, most probably. The question is for how long the human species, and other species as well, can sustain it.

In the scenario that has just been described, the environmental catastrophes could occur relatively soon, in a matter of decades. They have been described in the first chapter, and note that, except for possible tipping point phenomena that may suddenly break up, it is not so much the environment's rebellion that will most likely kill many of us, but the inter-human conflicts that worsening life conditions will inevitably trigger.

It is therefore very important not to lose sight of the sustainability goal. Ignoring it now, in the pursuit of a myopic notion of human development, may not just jeopardize the opulence of a distant, technically more advanced, future. It may kill many of our children and grandchildren.

THE AUTHORITARIAN SCENARIO

The rise of populism in the rich countries makes the Apartheid scenario more likely than the "end-of-history" scenario, but it also gives it a rather mediocre outlook as far as achieving serious progress on the freedom and democracy front is concerned. Here is, now, another scenario in which democracy and freedom are seriously curtailed while some success is achieved with respect to the other goals.

In this scenario, authoritarian governments flourish in many countries of the world, and, led by China and perhaps India and Indonesia, they initiate several important shifts in global policies. Such shifts are partly explained by the fact that these authoritarian governments are less myopic than ordinary democratic legislatures, and are very concerned about the long-term threats to regime stability generated by development gaps and environmental degradation.

First, they strongly support economic development, in particular via a strong push for technology transfers and the building of regional development banks that bypass the traditional channels of global investment. Intellectual property rights are put under severe limitations with the purpose of enabling regional industrial giants to develop. Capital flows are likewise put under control in order to avoid financial crises induced by volatile movements. They have learned the lessons of two large financial crises (the 1997 Asian crisis and the 2007 financial crash), and noted that the countries that controlled foreign capital flows and their banking system were much more immune to global financial risks. Reluctantly, global financial institutions adjust to these initiatives and agree to let funds go through these new banks, since increased controls on capital flows curb the flow of large direct investments in poor countries. Asian investment in poor regions of the world, including Africa, surges and helps many countries to develop some basic industrial capacity and modernize their agriculture.

Second, these regimes adopt voluntarist policies on population control. These policies are not always welcomed by poor populations, for whom children are an important resource for additional revenue and for support in old age. Some authoritarian interventions with strong penalties for the second and especially the third child are implemented, but are also accompanied by a strong push for the education of girls, crushing the resistance of traditionalist cultures still dominated by patriarchy. It is widely accepted that the education of girls is a powerful way to accelerate the reduction of the fertility rate, because it gives women greater status, more access to jobs and resources, and therefore greater control over the number of children in their families.

Figure 4.7 shows the increase in population projected by the UN under different assumptions about the demography. The continuation of current fertility rates (around 2.45 children per woman at the world level, with wide disparities across regions) leads to an explosive nightmare, the higher exponential curve on the graph. The

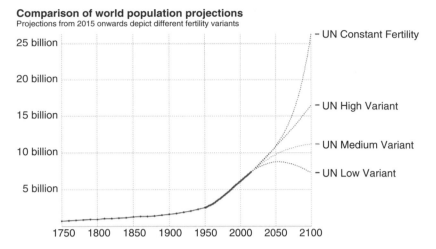

Comparison of world population projections
Projections from 2015 onwards depict different fertility variants

FIGURE 4.7 Population Projections Worldwide
Source: Our World in Data.

more reasonable scenarios all predict a reduction of the fertility rates with the "demographic transition" (joint reduction in mortality and natality) unfolding in the poorer countries in which it has not yet happened. The scenario in which the population decreases after 2050 involves a world fertility rate going durably below 2, as has already been observed in many developed countries.

The authoritarian scenario we consider here might be able to push the world toward the lower population path, which would be really a great help in the goal of preserving the environment and the climate. It is estimated that an increase of 1 percent in the population numbers leads to an increase in CO_2 emissions that ranges between 1 percent and 2.5 percent (O'Neill et al. 2012; Casey and Galor 2017). The difference between the high and the low UN-predicted populations in 2100 is almost 10 billion people, representing 144 percent of the 6.8 billion people of the low path! Reducing the population would go a long way toward alleviating the climate change threat.

But that would not be enough, because population would continue to increase until 2050, and development by emerging economies would potentially make industrial emissions soar, as well as methane emissions due to agriculture and especially cattle raising. While methane is a short-lived gas (half of it is decomposed in about twelve years, unlike CO_2, which is very stable and remains for millennia), its greenhouse effect is much stronger than that of CO_2 and therefore a continuous increase in methane emissions in the century would have a strong impact on temperatures. It would be especially problematic if the developing world adopted the meat-rich diet of the developed countries. That is where the authoritarian governments, in this scenario, intervene by strongly curbing meat production and educating people to adopt a better diet that is both more environmentally friendly and healthier. One recent study found that "transitioning toward more plant-based diets that are in line with standard dietary guidelines could reduce global mortality by 6–10 percent and food-related greenhouse gas emissions by 29–70 percent compared with a reference scenario in 2050" (Springmann et al. 2016). Given that food-related greenhouse gas emissions are estimated to account for about a quarter of the total emissions, this is a substantial impact. One potential adverse side-effect of this policy is that the money saved on health costs could be spent on other goods with serious environmental impact, thus leading to what is called a "rebound" effect, i.e. an increase of greenhouse gas emissions ultimately happening due to a policy that initially reduces them. Here again, the strong arm of the states of this scenario can prevent the rebound effect on greenhouse emissions by controlling the use of saved resources.

Yet another facet of the strong-arm policies is witnessed in the domain of urban design. Both in new cities and in the remodeling of old cities, the dominant policy in this scenario consists in curbing urban sprawl and car use, and promoting dense habitat that reduces the length of commutes and improves energy saving in cold areas – though it sometimes creates problems of "heat islands" in hot parts of the world, tackled by combining as much vegetation as possible with buildings. Strong incentives are also put on having people work from home. These policies involve an authoritarian approach to land use and real estate markets that is hardly available to more liberal governments, except perhaps in the case of designing new cities. As it turns out, while the transition is hard for the traditional suburban dwellers used to wandering around in their cars – the typical characters of the American movies of the late twentieth century – the new generation adapts quickly to the denser habitat and community life is quite thriving in certain neighborhoods, fostered by good public space for pedestrians and children and proximity of shopping facilities where contacts are frequent among locals.

What is worrisome about this scenario is that there is no guarantee that the authoritarian governments, which wisely but perhaps not humanely force an energy-frugal lifestyle on the population with long-term stability in mind, will be wise in all respects and measured in their use of authority. The historically proven side-effect of authoritarianism is abuse of power, on any sort of occasion, followed by an escalating level of protest and repression leading to severe disruption and serious waste of resources, not to mention the terrible cost in human rights violations and human lives. On a less dramatic level, authoritarianism is also associated with a greater degree of corruption than is democracy (Kolstad and Wiig 2016), perhaps due to the lack of checks and balances, implying a lack of transparency, in particular with a lower freedom of the press. While corruption may sometimes lubricate the system, allowing those with pressing demands to get priority attention from a resource-limited bureaucracy, it generally distracts resources and generates terrible inefficiencies. The idea that authoritarian governments can be more effective at forcing lifestyle changes toward a greener economy therefore hinges on the not-so-plausible assumption that corruption and violence will not impede such achievements.

Democracy may be a very imperfect system, but it is the best, when combined with a strong rule of law, to minimize the likelihood of such an escalation of social unrest and violence. Democratic regimes can slide into authoritarianism and have occasional bursts

THE BIG CHALLENGE 103

of protest, especially when social cohesion falls apart and part of the population feels that the social contract has been broken by the elites. We are now in this dangerous moment in many developed countries and a few emerging economies. But, still, democracies are not just the most promising beacon of freedom, they are the *only* system that provides a reasonable guarantee of preserving minimal individual and collective, economic, social, and cultural freedoms in the long run.

TRENDS AND OPPORTUNITIES

It is tempting to ask which of the three scenarios is most likely, and recent developments toward reduced international cooperation and a leaner welfare state under austerity policies may suggest that the Apartheid scenario has already started. But reading the scenarios as predictions would be mistaken. They are only warning signs, glimpses of what could happen if certain trends were left to dominate the future.

But one should completely abandon a deterministic, mechanistic conception of history. Such conceptions are always popular because they have a sense of gravity. Influenced by Hegel, Marx thought he could develop a theory of "historical materialism," where the study of the deep trends of the economic system would explain most social phenomena, including people's "ideology." He envisioned that humanity would free itself from this economic determinism only in the era of abundance inaugurated by the advent of communism, giving an economic twist to Hegel's aphorism that "the owl of Minerva spreads its wings only with the falling of the dusk." One finds less prophetic but similarly deterministic accents in Piketty's (2014) doom theory of the intrinsic tendency of capitalism to let capital take the advantage and generate explosive inequalities, unless some strong taxation policies are enacted. And, on a much less respectable but much more frightening level, we hear that a key adviser of the US President is inspired by a fantasy theory that history goes by cycles of crises, war, and redemption, the current period being the beginning of a new war phase.

Historical determinism is utterly wrong. There are always many opportunities to make history turn in various directions, and opportunities have always been present even in Antiquity, when the genius or madness of a few leaders could determine the fate of a city or kingdom. The interesting feature of the current period is that there has never been such a combination of grave global threats and tremendous opportunities, both generated by the success of human development. We may not be in the era of abundance, and communism as imagined by Marx is not around the corner, but we can certainly feel collectively empowered by our material and intellectual resources to consciously make key choices that may drive our population and the planet either over the cliff or to a brighter future.

It has been argued in this chapter that the key to a brighter future is to combine progress on the three fronts of equity, sustainability, and freedom. And three ways have been described, among many, in which humanity can fail in this somewhat daunting task. Now is the time to explore, in the second part of this book, how it can succeed.

PART II　**Acting for Social Progress**

5   In Search of a New "Third Way"

The first part of this book has shown that, after great achievements in the past centuries, pursuing "business as usual" is just impossible in the twenty-first century, unless we want to exacerbate tensions that could jeopardize the gains accumulated over the past half-century and destroy, or at least dramatically harm, the human species and many other species with it. Moreover, any way out of this predicament must jointly pursue the three goals of equity, sustainability, and freedom. While this challenge is daunting, it also offers a unique opportunity to rethink and improve the basic structure of society. Actually, it appears that only a significantly better society can tackle the challenge.

This immediately raises the following questions: How can this be achieved? What needs to be changed and what can be preserved? Who should do what? To answer such questions, we will proceed in three steps.

First, it is important to understand why the old ideological perspectives about capitalism and socialism, about the market and the government, are now obsolete, and how recent concepts developed by social sciences provide a much better way to understand what makes people thrive or struggle as they navigate the social system throughout their lives. This is the topic of this chapter, defending the project of seeking an alternative way, beyond capitalism and socialism.

Second, one needs to explore concrete alternatives and examine how the key institutions of society can be reformed. The focus in the next chapters will be on the market, the corporation, the welfare state, and politics. Concrete proposals will be made about how to reform them and garner their strengths toward the three goals of equity, sustainability, and freedom.

Finally, one needs to identify a strategy for change and a set of actors, the "change-makers" who can push for the desired transformations. This will be the topic of the concluding chapter. The key message will be that transformative change has to involve bottom-up initiatives as well as – and probably more than – top-down direction. So, the concluding chapter will invite every reader to become a change-maker.

SOCIALISM AND PROPERTY

In the Marxist perspective, the history of societies has been a succession of contrivances enabling certain elite groups to amass advantages by exploiting a working multitude. Capitalism is just the latest of such systems, with ordinary workers being exploited by investors and employers. The process which generates exploitation in capitalism involves the labor market where labor is exchanged for money, and in which workers accept contracts that leave a profit to the wealthy elite. The owners of the "means of production" hire workers and extract "surplus value" by paying for their work at less than its full value.

This vision of capitalism implies a focus on the distribution of ownership of the "means of production." It identifies private property as the source of all problems, since every private owner can exploit labor simply by hiring services on the labor market. The list of reforms advocated at the end the Communist Manifesto is worth revisiting:[1]

1. Abolition of property in land and application of all rents of land to public purposes.
2. A heavy progressive or graduated income tax.
3. Abolition of all rights of inheritance.
4. Confiscation of the property of all emigrants and rebels.

[1] This list is discussed in the IPSP (2018a, chapter 8).

5. Centralization of credit in the hands of the state, by means of a national bank with State capital and an exclusive monopoly.
6. Centralization of the means of communication and transport in the hands of the State.
7. Extension of factories and instruments of production owned by the State; the bringing into cultivation of waste-lands, and the improvement of the soil generally in accordance with a common plan.
8. Equal liability of all to work. Establishment of industrial armies, especially for agriculture.
9. Combination of agriculture with manufacturing industries; gradual abolition of all the distinction between town and country.
10. Free education for all children in public schools. Abolition of children's factory labor in its present form. Combination of education with industrial production.

This list is full of items that aim at expropriating wealth and nationalizing capital. Some of them have been implemented since then. The public central bank, progressive income taxation, and public schooling, together with some public utilities, have now become routine (though not without ups and downs). But the other items appear either unappealing or outright frightening – the idea of an "industrial army" is eerily reminiscent of the *Soldaten der Arbeit* that Bismarck imagined and Hitler and Stalin implemented. Conspicuously missing in the list are many now standard social programs like health insurance or public pensions.

What the Marxist approach failed to see is that private property is popular, and successful in generating economic and social progress, for a good reason. People need to plan their lives and to feel independent. When everything they consume comes from a common pot, two things happen. First, there is a natural tendency to free ride, by failing to contribute to the common pot and by taking too much from the pot, leading to the so-called "tragedy of the commons." Second, since the lack of incentives to contribute requires an "army" discipline at work, and the lack of incentives to be frugal requires rationing consumption goods, people then fall into a state of strong dependency on the guardians of the system, which runs against the natural desire

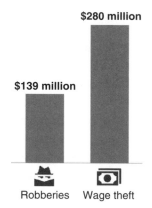

Widespread wage theft needs a stronger government response

Value of wage theft* compared with value of combined street, bank, gas station, and convenience store robberies, 2012

FIGURE 5.1 Wage Theft versus Mugging in the USA
Note: * Value of back wages illegally withheld by employers recovered by US Department of Labor in 2012.
Source: www.epi.org/publication/wage-theft-bigger-problem-theft-protect/.

of people to be in control of their lives. In contrast, private property provides owners with a sense of security and with incentives to create wealth diligently and to manage their property prudently.

The Marxist theory of exploitation also turns out to be flawed. Profit is not, in essence, stolen labor. Under normal conditions, it does reward the actual services of innovation, capital, and management. Sometimes profit is inflated by market power enabling firms to lower wages and raise prices. Sometimes undue advantage is taken of vulnerable workers who are forced to work without pay or are simply deprived of their due wages. Wage theft is estimated to be at least twice as important as street robberies in the USA, for instance (Figure 5.1). But not all profit is theft.

THIRD WAYS

While the Marxist doctrine has now been largely abandoned, it remains influential through a persistent focus on property (income or wealth) redistribution today in policy debates. But these debates can be framed as being about something that is neither pure capitalism nor pure socialism. The search for a "third way" has been a favorite pastime of thinkers and policy-makers alike.

There have been two different popular conceptions of the third way, and a less popular third one that we will ultimately highlight. They are not exclusive and, in the coming chapters, we will argue for combining them in an appropriate way.

The most traditional one theorizes the welfare state as the embodiment of the third way. The welfare state is conceived of as a redistributive machine which curbs market inequalities between profits and wages as well as between high wages and low wages. Progressive taxation creates a mixed capitalist system in which inequalities remain moderate, while the economy continues to operate under the canons of the capitalist market system. Minimum wage laws also contribute to maintaining the living standards of the least skilled workers at a decent level, inducing firms to adopt technologies and methods which make labor sufficiently productive.

The second conception of the third way still gives a prominent role to the welfare state, but with a different aim. Instead of curbing inequalities *after* the market (through taxes and transfers) or *in* the market (through minimum wages, rent regulation, and similar price controls), the goal is to prepare individuals *for* the market by giving them the means to compete successfully, through the provision of good school and university education, good health care, and similar services. This is the third way conceptualized by Anthony Giddens and which inspired Tony Blair. As Giddens wrote, "the cultivation of human potential should as far as possible replace 'after the event' redistribution" (1998, p. 101). This approach, more than the previous one, is very concerned with letting the market operate as efficiently as possible in order to preserve competitiveness in a globalized world.

Of course, most welfare states combine the two approaches, and some have additional features, such as the Scandinavian countries in which the state also encourages central bargaining between labor and business interests so as to define a set of wage levels that keep the economy productive and competitive while limiting inequalities. Chapter 7 will examine the welfare state in greater detail.

There is a third "third way" that is less well known. It does not directly involve the state but aims at reforming the productive institutions themselves through the development of stakeholder-driven corporations and non-standard firms such as cooperatives. This tradition goes back to early debates among socialists, opposing those who wanted the state to seize property and protect workers to those who wanted to put the workers in control of new, worker-owned, productive associations. The "statists" won the internal political battle in the left and the other brand ("guild socialism") faded. The latter tradition is currently being revived in the thriving "third sector" of cooperatives, social enterprises, and similarly mutual ventures which espouse different principles than the mere pursuit of profit. The cooperative sector alone now involves more than 1 billion worker-members and user-members throughout the world (Table 5.1), and the total number of its worker-members and producer-members is more than twice the number of employees in transnational corporations (UNRISD 2016). Its advocates argue that it provides an alternative to capitalism, although, generally, this sector is seen as meant to supplement the standard economy, not to replace it.

However, some thinkers such as John Stuart Mill or Nobel Prize winner James Meade did think of an alternative to capitalism involving the replacement of capitalist relations by real partnerships in which workers would have a say in the governance of productive associations, in their capacity of work providers, not as owners of capital. In this form of the third way, labor would hire capital, instead of the opposite as is the case in capitalism. Meade (1964) imagined a complex formula by which workers would receive shares giving them rights to part of the value added generated by the firm. While his formula was never really experimented with, the idea of a democratic form of corporate governance involving the relevant

Table 5.1 *Cooperative Employment and Membership Worldwide*

	No. of coops	Cooperative employment			Total employment (A+B+C)	User-members (D)	Total members (B+C+D)
		Employees (A)	Worker-members (B)	Producer-members (C)			
Europe (37)	221,960	4,710,595	1,554,687	9,157,350	15,422,632	152,064,608	162,776,645
Africa (35)	375,375	1,939,836	37,836	20,410,298	22,387,970	33,638,298	54,086,432
Asia (33)	2,156,219	7,426,760	8,573,775	219,247,186	235,247,721	320,130,233	547,951,194
America (39)	181,378	1,896,257	982,285	3,237,493	6,116,035	417,580,396	421,800,174
Oceania (12)	2,391	75,438	0	147,071	222,509	30,696,144	30,843,215
Grand total (156)	2,937,323	16,048,836	11,148,583	252,199,398	279,396,867	954,109,679	1,217,457,660

Source: Hyung-sik Eum (2017).

stakeholders and especially the workers has become popular in certain schools of management. This issue will be discussed further in the next chapter.

NOT JUST A MATTER OF RESOURCES

What is especially interesting about this third "third way" is that it does not leave the institutions of the market economy untouched, and relies on a transformation of the social relations within a core economic institution, the productive company. It reflects a broader perspective than the traditional socialist focus on property, and considers the possibility of redistributing power without redistributing wealth or expropriating the owners. It also reflects a concern for power and social status that is absent from the conceptions of a third way centered on the welfare state and the distribution of assets and resources.

.   It is often overlooked that private property is not naturally given but is an institution shaped by norms and laws. What you are allowed to do with your property can vary a lot. In particular, the acceptability of using wealth to buy power over workers, citizens' votes, influence over politicians, media leverage, social prestige, or a clean soul is contestable, and in different contexts these practices have been variably considered perfectly normal, completely unacceptable, and all nuances in between. Therefore, the key battle for social progress may not be so much about redistributing wealth as about delineating the rights of wealth.

In most of the examples of contested uses of wealth just cited, the conversion of resources into power or status is at stake. The distribution of power and the distribution of status are essential aspects of the quality of a society. The socialist tradition, obsessed with property, has been less concerned about inequalities in other dimensions, thus paving the way to strongly hierarchical and authoritarian institutions, and history has shown how blindness about an important dimension of social justice can completely undermine grand ideals and produce terrible human suffering.

Now that the socialist dream of collective property has been largely abandoned, the debate about social progress has shifted to the more pragmatic question of the degree and form of government intervention in the market economy, but remains centered on the redistribution of resources. While it cannot be denied that this is a central question, it is regrettable how narrowly this question is framed in typical public debates, and how this may hide the most promising reforms from sight.

First of all, the economy is only partly a market affair. The most important economic activities actually happen in the family and in the firm (without forgetting the government agencies and public institutions that provide public goods and services as well as essential infrastructures). The family and the firm shield individuals from market competition and enable them to cooperate, as groups, toward common success in the outside world (where, indeed, they go on the market). Why is this important? Because people's wellbeing depends in crucial ways of what happens in these groups and organizations. Focusing the question of social progress on the virtues and flaws of the market is missing how people flourish or struggle in their families, workplaces, schools, and so on.

For instance, an essential phenomenon that accompanied women's increasing participation in the labor market has been a change in their share of resources but also their relative status and control in the household, and a – still insufficient – redistribution of household chores among spouses. The persistent pay gap between men and women on the labor market is an important issue, but not just for distributional equity. It is connected to what happens within the household in terms of the status, power, and independence of women.[2]

---

[2] See IPSP (2018c, chapter 17) for a detailed analysis of how women's situation in the family has changed in relation to changes in the labor market and in government policy.

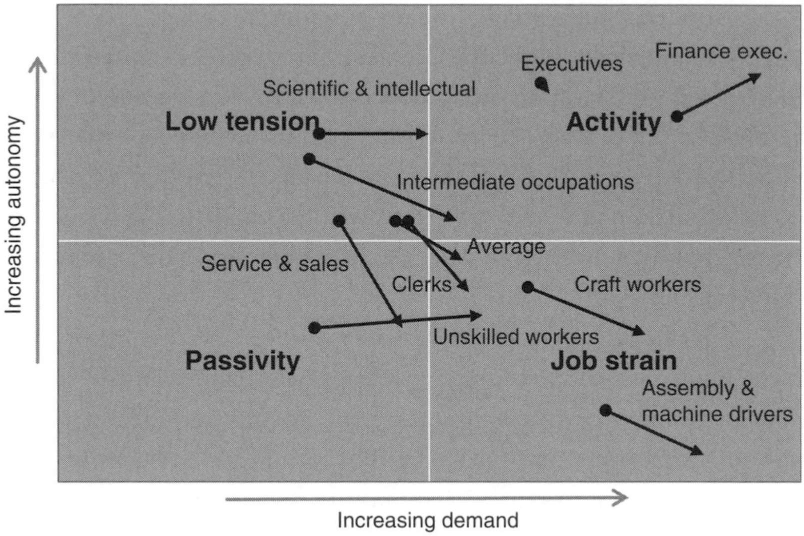

FIGURE 5.2 Job Strain in Europe (1995–2010)
Note: Black arrows represent direction of change over the time period.
Source: Askenazy (2016).

JOB STRAIN IN EUROPE, DEATHS IN THE USA

The workplace provides another central example of the importance of control and social status. A job does not just give you an income. It also gives you a social status and it occupies you most of the week, putting you in a hierarchy that shapes how much control over your work life you have. When things go wrong in the workplace, you do not just worry about keeping your job and your income. You may lose your dignity, or your health under stress. It does indeed appear that job stress has increased in the recent decades. Interesting tools for measuring stress at work have been developed by labor sociologists Johannes Siegrist, Robert Karasek, and Töres Theorell. They look at job quality and job strain in terms of a mismatch between demand and reward (broken contract) and a harmful combination of high demand and low autonomy on the job (see Figure 5.2).[3]

[3] See IPSP (2018a, chapter 7) for additional explanations about the approaches and measures.

That economic problems undermine more than people's living standards is vividly shown by Princeton economists Anne Case and Angus Deaton (2015, 2017), who observe that mortality rates for middle-aged white lower-class Americans have stopped improving and are rising again, while the rates for other social, ethnic, and age groups continue the downward trend (although a very recent upswing seems to affect black people). European countries, at the same time, have recorded a continuous improvement. The immediate causes for the US mortality crisis seemed to be primarily drugs (including painkillers), alcohol, and suicide. Case and Deaton show that the deeper causes or correlates seem to be not just stalling incomes, but also reduced labor participation (due to discouragement and sickness), lower marriage rate, increased family breakdowns, and greater difficulties socializing with friends.

These data reveal that social trends are much more worrisome than they look when seen through the economic lens. The income of blue-collar workers may have stagnated on average, but these people have a perception of their situation which is much bleaker and encompasses the social dislocation, the loss of status and recognition, the loss of control, and the health and death toll that ensue. Where economic statistics display stagnation, people's concrete experience is of a clear deterioration of their situation. The anger expressed by crowds and voters in many Western democracies over the past decade probably has a lot to do with this feeling of a worsening trend contrasting with the self-satisfaction of an establishment which primarily looks at macroeconomic data.

What does this tell us about seeking a better society? It shows that while jobs and wages matter a lot, what happens *within* families, communities, and workplaces is also very important. Moreover, it is important in two ways. First, a fairer distribution of resources, status, and control in these collectives directly benefits people's ability to flourish, to plan their lives, and it fosters their self-esteem and their health. Second, altering the distribution of power changes the governance structure and alters the decisions made, with many additional consequences. Households where women have greater control take greater care of the education of children and especially of girls, inducing a virtuous circle. Firms where the stakeholders have a greater say have a narrower wage gap and are more socially and environmentally responsible, as will be discussed in the next chapters of this book.

VOICES OF THE POOR

If you are not convinced that a focus on the market and on the redistribution of economic resources is too narrow to explore the way to a better society, listen to the voice of the poorest people. One might believe that those who are the most deprived of resources should be the most focused on this dimension. But this is not the case. "The worst thing about living in extreme poverty is the contempt, that they treat you like you are worthless, that they look at you with disgust and fear and that they even treat you like an enemy. We and our children experience this every day, and it hurts us, humiliates us and makes us live in fear and shame," says Edilberta Béjar from Peru in ATD (2013, p. 39). And the degree of constraint imposed by others, including agencies supposed to help, is also crushing, for instance when children are taken away for placement in foster care or when conditional aid involves intrusive monitoring. As an activist from Senegal says:

> Today's society acts with arrogance by thinking that it can bring an end to suffering solely by sharing material goods. It thinks that it can end poverty and exclusion with the accumulation of goods. This prevents the world from having to think about the essential issue, which is the effort of each and every person to create the conditions for liberty and liberation in a land of extreme poverty.
>
> *(ATD 2013, p. 54)*

These quotes come from a report by ATD, an NGO which has always argued that the poor should be the agents of their own liberation. Another organization also proves that these ideals of dignity and emancipation are widespread in the world: the Self-Employed Women Association (SEWA) in India, which has more than 2 million members who are among the poorest women. It works as a union association fostering initiatives in training, finance, and various forms of management support.

"The work of SEWA is based on the core beliefs that economic empowerment leads to social justice, that work must contribute to growth and development of others, and that the decentralization of economic ownership and production creates a more just society" (IPSP 2018a, chapter 8). What is especially interesting about their approach is that it links empowerment not just to accessing resources but also to improving status, self-esteem, and dignity. Moreover, inspired by Indian thought, there is an important focus on relations, both among people and between people and nature, with a sense of reciprocity and a special attention to democratic proceedings and making sure that the weakest have their say.

In other words, their philosophy is very much about improving relations and about providing access to knowledge, control, status, and resources. They promote decentralization and communal work, with the idea that communities in control of their own livelihood, locally, take better care of the environment and become more self-resilient. They also aim at giving greater recognition to non-monetary work that serves useful functions in the life of the community.

Based on this philosophy, SEWA has developed important initiatives in finance with its own cooperative bank, in training with a management school for micro-entrepreneurs, in food security with its distribution chain, and in new communication technologies for the dissemination of information on prices and assistance in transactions. Millions of Indians have benefited from these initiatives.

COMPETITION VERSUS COOPERATION

If the search for a better society should not be focused on, or limited to, the redistribution of resources by the government, in what directions should the search go? Recent developments in social sciences, as reflected in the analyses of the IPSP report, suggest the following vision of what makes society enhance or undermine human flourishing.

People's wellbeing depends not just on their economic living standards, but also on the quality of their social relations. We are social beings, and our flourishing, even in the most individualistic cultures, is deeply shaped by social interactions.[4]

Since its origins, humans have congregated in groups in which they developed cooperation in order to better compete against the outside world. Competition for leadership and other advantages has also plagued these groups' histories, but humans are among the most cooperative species, and have probably developed this capacity through an evolutionary process that selected the most effective groups, i.e. those in which cooperation worked the best.

The mix of competition and cooperation has evolved throughout history and remains different in various parts of the world. In some countries, children are raised in a patriotic vision of dedication to the common goals of the nation, whereas in others, personal success is promoted and individualistic competition starts early at school. Local communities and extended families keep strong ties of solidarity in some places, whereas in others solidarity does not extend much beyond the nuclear family, or is shared between the nuclear family and the welfare state. As explained earlier, firms are organizations in which workers and other contributors cooperate to produce and sell on the market. A market transaction is itself a cooperative venture between the traders (the common goal being to reach an agreement and mutually benefit from the transaction).

In general, cooperation is more conducive to social relations of good quality than competition, even if cooperation does not eliminate conflicts of interest, since, in a cooperative venture, sharing contributions and rewards pits people against each other to some

---

[4] See chapters 2 and 8 of IPSP (2018a) for analyses of the determinants of wellbeing.

extent. A cooperative ethos can also be oppressive. One of the authors of this book, after a public lecture on cooperatives, heard from a former cooperative member that the mutual pressure to work hard was too high ("colleagues would call you at home when you were sick, asking you to come back"). Cooperation among some actors may also be harmful to others, as in market cartels that hurt customers. But in general, incentives obtained by a cooperative setting are more condu-cive to human flourishing than competitive emulation, and they also enhance the level of trust and the circulation of information, making the group more effective. Therefore, encouraging cooperation rather than competition within families, communities, schools, and firms is generally considered good advice.[5]

THE WEB OF SOCIAL INTERACTIONS

While the competition–cooperation distinction is useful, it does not provide a sufficiently fine-grained description of the various patterns of social relations. This book is not the place to provide a general theory of social relations, but here are typical examples of social relations that go badly (and can happen both in competitive and cooperative contexts), and should be avoided as much as possible when seeking to design better institutions.

Let us start with bad relations involving imbalance in power and control. People can be deprived of sufficient control over their life in three ways at least. They can be *subordinated*, like the wife in the patriarchal family and the worker in the traditional firm. But they can also be *dependent* without being subordinated, when their situation depends on external forces they don't control, like the welfare recipient who is not sure to receive steady support from a

---

[5] An IPSP survey performed on a representative sample of the US population in 2017 shows a clear preference for cooperation. On average people feel better in cooperative situations (less stressed and angry, more elated and excited, equally focused), and a majority of respondents think that increasing cooperation in their life would make it better overall (55%), less stressful (59%), and more pleasant (57%), while only a small proportion think it would worsen it on these fronts (respectively, 10%, 12%, and 12%).

capricious administration and is therefore unable to make long-term plans, or the women who cannot safely walk in the streets at certain hours. Finally, they can be *obligated* by duties imposed on them, like the last daughter in the family who is supposed to remain single and stay with her parents to take care of them in their old age, or the cooperative worker mentioned earlier, who can hardly take a day of sick leave.

Problems with social status provide another set of cases in which people may be deprived of dignity. First, this can happen through humiliation and *shame*, as described by the poor quoted earlier in this chapter. It is indeed very problematic that many welfare policies that are supposed to help the poor actually undermine their dignity in this way. Many firms also treat their workers in a humiliating way, for instance in the way in which they submit them to urinal drug tests during hiring procedures. Second, people can be discriminated against by being *excluded*, shunned, and ostracized, like the Roma people in Europe or the Dalit caste in India. Third, discrimination can also mean being included but in *inferior* social roles, as in the hierarchy of jobs of public work in many countries, which often follows strict racial lines.

All these forms of oppressive social relations can be combined in concrete situations. For instance, consider the very frequent case of a blue-collar female worker being sexually harassed by a foreman.[6] This can take a *humiliating* form (colleagues laugh), conveying a sense of extreme *subordination* and being associated with the idea that female workers have an *inferior* role in the organization. It can also be linked to blackmailing about promotion, exacerbating the *dependence* of the subordinate on the good will of the superior.

Given the increasing importance of higher education and knowledge in the economy and in politics, the circulation of information provides other important examples of harmful social interactions.

---

[6] See www.lemonde.fr/societe/article/2017/11/23/violences-sexuelles-chez-les-ouvrieres-la-peur-de-perdre-son-travail_5219215_3224.html.

The lack of transparency in the governance of organizations is often providing cover for questionable practices, and the growing role of whistleblowers has revealed how transformative transparency can be, generally, for the better. The distortion of information is also profoundly impactful, notably in politics, and the growing concern about fake news is now reviving the old fight against propaganda. In summary, people can be either *deprived* of information, as is the case for many women not receiving education or being dominated in their family, as well as for most workers left in the dark by their employer about decisions that deeply affect their professional and personal life; or they can be *deceived*, as when propagandists seek to induce electoral behavior that is not in the true interest of the citizens.

These are just a few examples of a myriad ways in which social interactions can be harmful. What should be emphasized is that what happens in one particular interaction influences other interactions. It has already been mentioned that a change in women's participation in the labor market (from exclusion to inclusion, and toward higher status jobs) has changed their situation in the household, giving them not just more resources but also greater control and better status. These spillovers between different interactions lead people to make tradeoffs. People accept a bad job when it gives them sufficient resources to afford a divorce and acquire greater independence from an oppressive family. Welfare support may generate dependence with respect to social workers or government policy, but may simultaneously improve the recipient's ability to bargain on the labor market and obtain more resources, greater control, and better status. People may accept the humiliation of certain paternalistic and conspicuous forms of welfare support (like food stamps) for the sake of giving their kids a better education. Or, conversely, they may avoid sending their kids to school, somehow excluding themselves from society, in order to hide their misery and avoid seeing their kids sent away to foster care.

A fair society is one in which social interactions are, as much as possible, devoid of all of these bad interaction patterns that undermine people's dignity. It is a society that avoids making people face hard tradeoffs where they must trade their dignity for other advantages.

PROMOTING SOCIAL JUSTICE

There are two ways in which bad social interactions can be fought. One way consists in providing people with the assets that enable them to navigate the various interactions with success. Supporting school and university access and lifelong learning, as well as providing health care, makes workers stronger on the labor market, income security makes beneficiaries stronger at home and at work, accurate information makes citizens stronger when they participate in politics, granting LGBTQI people the right to marry and have children makes them stronger and better included in their community, distributing income support to women may enhance their control over household expenditures, and so on.

The other way of curbing bad interactions consists in changing the rules of the game in the various settings and organizations in which interactions take place. Imposing strict limitations on market concentration and on banking activities protects consumers and borrowers, democratizing (i.e. sharing power and information in) public organizations makes citizens' voice more effective, and democratizing firms gives workers much greater dignity. It is harder to change the rules of the game in families and in communities, but this can be achieved through pressure by the relevant stakeholders.[7]

The two ways are not exclusive and can reinforce each other, or produce virtuous circles. For instance, paying cash transfers to women can enhance their power and status, and little by little contribute to changing the norms and traditions governing gender roles in the family.

---

[7] The idea that it is important to think in terms of reforming the rules of the game is defended in Stiglitz (2015) and World Bank (2017).

Equipped with these concepts, let us now revisit the socialist and third-way visions of a better society. The third ways that involve the state redistributing resources after the market, or investing in people's assets before the market, primarily rely on the idea of supporting people with assets that enhance their ability to succeed. The redistribution of resources after the market enables them to succeed as consumers (and as family and community members, if the stigma of support is not too harmful), whereas the provision of assets for the market also enables them to succeed as workers (and largely avoids stigma issues). In contrast, the socialist platform and the third "third way" aim at changing the rules of the game in a deeper way. The socialist platform is flawed because it replaces the privilege of wealth by authoritarian schemes that generate highly deteriorated social interactions. The third "third way" that seeks to develop cooperation and enhance the dignity of workers and citizens by reforming the firm and other social institutions is much more promising in light of its likely consequences on social relations. Similar ideas can guide reforms of the welfare state and the way it relates to its beneficiaries.

Along these lines, the following chapters explore how changes in the market and the corporation, the welfare state and the political sphere, can bring us closer to such a fair society.

6   Reforming Capitalism

In the previous chapter, we have argued that one should go beyond the old-fashioned opposition between private property and socialism and pursue reforms of the prevailing institutions of the market, the corporation, and the state, to open a third way toward a more humane society. In this chapter, we focus on the central institutions of modern capitalism: the corporation, markets, and financial institutions.

Max Weber powerfully defined the paradoxical nature of modern capitalism. He saw it as "identical with the pursuit of profit and forever renewed profit, by means of continuous, rational, capitalistic enterprise" (Weber 2001). But he also insisted that the sort of life associated with this modern Western rational capitalism appeared, "from the point of view of the happiness of or utility to the single individual entirely transcendental and absolutely irrational." What was irrational here, according to him? The fact that "man is dominated by the making of money, by acquisition as the ultimate purpose of life," rather than by having "economic acquisition as simply subordinated to man as the means for the satisfaction of his material needs." Can we overcome this paradox and reform capitalism in a way that would allow us to harness economic rationality in the service of human flourishing?

An empirical and historical exploration tells us that there has been great diversity, across time and space, in the forms capitalism has taken. This diversity remains even if one restricts attention to Max Weber's conception of *modern rational capitalism*. How can one describe the contemporary dominant ideal-type of capitalism? This form of capitalism has a number of striking features. First, we find the large joint stock corporation as the dominant actor in complex and often multinational value chains. Second, the corporate legal structure comes with a separation of ownership and control that has fostered the emergence and development of management as a (quasi-)profession and even as an industry. Third, a striking evolution of corporate and managerial capitalism since the late 1970s has been its coupling with increasing calls for market solutions. Fourth, this expansive marketization has co-evolved with the growth of finance as a dominant actor in the capitalist constellation and, perhaps even more significantly, as a hegemonic culture of contemporary economies, societies, and polities. This chapter explores these striking features and some of the dynamics that have led to contemporary capitalism as we know it. In the process, it identifies a number of problematic or even worrisome trends and it suggests paths through which we should question and reform our contemporary capitalist ideal-type in order to align it better with a progressive agenda that gives priority to human needs and aspirations.

REFORMING THE GOVERNANCE AND PURPOSE OF THE CORPORATION

The corporation is a constitutive element of contemporary capitalism and an institution that we take for granted today. Still, its central role in economic production, organization, and exchange is relatively recent. Until the mid-nineteenth century, corporate charters and their associated prerogatives were granted by the sovereign or the state as counterparts for risk-taking in the service of public interest. The diffusion of general incorporation acts that essentially "privatized" the corporate regime was a legal development that took place in most countries during the second half of the nineteenth century.

The contemporary features of the corporation took time to emerge and become accepted. In its modern legal form, the corporation is indeed quite remarkable. First, it is treated in legal terms as an artificial individual. As such it has a legal existence independent of its members and holds rights and obligations in its own name. Second, the modern corporation translates ownership into the holding of shares and, as a consequence, induces a decoupling of ownership and management. In its modern form, corporate ownership tends to be dispersed and shares are easily transferable and marketable. This peculiar status and this ownership pattern imply that the corporation can survive the life span of its original shareholders, potentially existing in perpetuity. Moreover, as a legal entity the corporation is protected by strong asset-partitioning and entity-shielding – meaning that the creditors of the owners or shareholders have no claims over the assets of the corporate legal entity. Finally, and quite crucially, modern corporate share ownership is associated with the principle of limited liability. Shareholders cannot be made liable for the debts and other liabilities of the corporation beyond the value of their holdings. Hence, the modern corporation could be described as the first "enhanced (artificial) individual": it has all the rights and prerogatives associated with legal personality while enjoying immortality and a striking limitation of its responsibility and liability.

Those features and prerogatives explain the success of the corporation as a legal form in the twentieth century. They have been identified as drivers of growth, risk-taking, entrepreneurship, and innovation. From the very beginning, however, the corporation and associated prerogatives aroused vocal opposition. Debates have focused on two main sets of issues: limited liability and its consequences, and the governance and purpose of the corporation.

Among the most violent early critics of the corporation we find no less than Adam Smith. In *An Inquiry into the Nature and Causes of the Wealth of Nations* (2012 [1776]), Smith argued that corporations tended to reduce or distort competition, to encourage speculation and embezzlement, to allow raw power and oppression, and to significantly weaken all forms of responsibility. In nineteenth-century debates around the generic association of limited liability and incorporation, opponents worried about the expansion of speculation, and of risky and fraudulent behaviors. Many arguments were moral ones, connecting "benefits and burdens," personal morality, and full responsibility:

> Advocates of limited responsibility proclaim that the scheme of Providence may be advantageously modified and that debts and obligations may be contracted which the debtors though they have the means shall not be bound to discharge.
>
> *(McCulloch 1856, p. 321)*

A contemporary take on those arguments underscores the moral hazard implications of limited liability. The extension of limited liability has encouraged risk-taking (and hence innovation and growth) *because* it created a situation of expanding de-responsibilization. Individuals took more risks precisely *because* they could reap rewards without having to bear the full costs. Limited liability has played, in other words, the role of a powerful insurance scheme, creating in the process a systemic moral hazard at the core of modern capitalism. From that perspective, the increased risk-taking associated with limited liability should be seen as a worrisome development likely to bring about great instability and regular crises and failures.

Similar concerns arose regarding governance. The structural decoupling of ownership and management in corporations has translated into multiple kinds of agency failures. This has produced, since the 1930s and the pioneering work of Adolf Berle and Gardiner Means, a rich and dense literature on corporate governance. There are two main interconnected issues in discussions on corporate governance. One is the nature of the relationship and the balance of power between managers and shareholders. The other is the legitimacy of considering other actors and their interests (beyond shareholders and managers) in governance systems and practices.

At the risk of over-simplifying, we have two extreme and partially opposed perspectives. From one standpoint, shareholders are defined as the "owners" of the corporation; managers are their agents and the only legitimate purpose of the corporation is to maximize the value for shareholders (Friedman 1970). A contrasting argument makes the point that shareholders do not own the corporation and that the responsibility of managers is to balance the interests of a diversity of stakeholders (Freeman 1984). Hence, the purpose of the corporation, from that perspective, is to serve the collective interest of the community of stakeholders it represents. In the case of large corporations with a quasi-global reach, this community becomes very broad and serving the collective interest of concerned stakeholders becomes nearly synonymous with serving the public interest and the common good.

Historically, corporate capitalism has oscillated between these two perspectives. Until the late 1970s, corporate capitalism was of a stakeholder type. The late 1970s saw a rise in the power of the shareholder – with a vengeance. Agency theory and its proposition that shareholders were the owners of the firm and managers their agents (Jensen and Meckling 1976) completely reshaped the theory and practice of corporate governance, turning corporations, in the process, into single-purpose entities that focused only on maximizing the return on investment for shareholders. This radical turn has become ideologically and structurally entrenched over the last forty years through its deep embeddedness in those institutions that train global elites – business schools and economics departments, but also law and public administration schools. As a clear consequence, the balance has tilted during that period in favor of capital and capital holders. The single-purpose focus of the contemporary corporation is clearly a major explanatory factor for increasing inequalities since the 1980s – with their disastrous social and political consequences. Hence, the pressing calls today for a return to a more balanced, stakeholder-type capitalism (Reich 2015).

On the basis of this assessment, there are at least three paths to explore: rethinking limited liability, transforming the governance and purpose of the corporation, and fostering the development of alternative forms of economic organization.

First, there is an urgent need to question the exorbitant privilege of limited liability. Historically, limited liability had been associated with a mission of public interest. Does generic limited liability make sense when corporations only serve private interest? There are different ways to think about a reform of limited liability, from more to less radical. One could think of outright abolition. One could want to rescind limited liability as a generic principle and return to exceptional granting on the basis of a common-good engagement. Finally, while keeping the principle of generic limited liability, one could envision the introduction of exceptions and expanded liability in certain sectors such as, for example, banking and the financial industry.

Second, it is high time to debunk the myth that corporations belong to shareholders. Legal scholars have by now convincingly shown that shareholders only own shares and hence are closer in their legitimacy claims to investors than to outright entity owners (Stout 2012). This should now translate into a transformation of corporate governance principles and even legal provisions, with a significant inflection toward a conception of the corporation as a commons serving a multiplicity of stakeholders and their interests. Various proposals have been made over time by many thinkers (starting from John Stuart Mill) about associating stakeholders, in particular workers, to decision-making in the corporation. The most natural formula would have a board composed of representatives of the various categories of stakeholders: shareholders, creditors, workers, suppliers, customers, local communities. Unlike the German system of co-determination which *de facto* gives a majority of power to shareholders, it would be important to avoid giving the absolute majority of power either to the shareholders or to the workers, in order to guarantee that the multiplicity of stakeholders' interests are taken into account.[1]

---

[1] See IPSP (2018a, chapter 8, and 2018c, chapter 21) for further discussion of democratic governance schemes.

This structural transformation should co-evolve with the reformulation of the purpose of the corporation. The proposition here is to move past the maximization of shareholder value and to enshrine multi-stakeholder interests or even common-good issues at the core of corporate purpose. Current experiments with the Benefit Corporation – a new corporate legal form that imposes a contribution to general public and stakeholder benefits – are interesting in this respect.[2] The challenge, though, would be not only to work on this at the margins of the system but to radically transform the philosophy that drives the running of our major corporations. In order to achieve this, one would need to bring along a change in the various national corporate or companies laws.

Third, there is a need to foster the development of conditions in which firms with alternative legal structures can thrive. We need to stimulate a rich ecology of economic undertakings. The power and wealth of contemporary corporations tend to stifle the deployment of alternatives. Cooperatives, partnerships, social entrepreneurship ventures, and collaborative and sharing economy platforms are important experiments from which the inclusive and progressive business models of tomorrow could and should emerge.

CORPORATE CAPITALISM, POWER, AND THREATS TO DEMOCRACY

By the early twenty-first century, corporate capitalism has reached unprecedented scale and scope. Corporations are involved in all dimensions of our lives, economies, and societies – the production and distribution of goods and services, insurance and banking, but also health, education, culture, sports, and even the production of national security, the running of prisons, or the organization of

[2] Thirty US states have authorized this new corporate legal form. In other parts of the world, mainstream corporations can apply for certification as B-Corp. This certification is run by a non-profit organization, B Lab, present in more than fifty countries, "that serves a global movement of people using business as a force for good." See www.bcorporation.net/.

protest and advocacy. This expansion of the reach of the corporation has often come with the transnationalization of operations and governance and with an unprecedented concentration of wealth and power. In turn, this concentration of power translates into direct and indirect threats to democracy and democratic justice.

There are many different ways to empirically measure and weigh the wealth and power of corporations. All figures, though, point to rapid internationalization over the last thirty years, sharply increasing business activity, revenues, and share of global trade, and striking concentration of capital, wealth, and resources through time. In 1990, the total number of transnational corporations was estimated at around 30,000. In 2010, the number of transnational parent corporations was estimated around 100,000 with about 900,000 foreign affiliates (Jaworek and Kuzel 2015, p. 57). Arguably figures vary from one year to the next but the overall trend, for the last ten years, is clear. If we compare nation-states and corporations by annual revenue, among the largest hundred entities, we find around sixty corporations and forty nation-states. Walmart, Apple, or Shell are richer, as measured by annual revenue, than Russia, Norway, or Belgium. More striking even: the world's top ten corporations have a combined revenue higher than that of the 180 "poorest" countries.[3]

The increasing wealth of multinational firms has translated into fast-growing profits over that period. For example, the value added of US multinational firms and their foreign affiliates was multiplied by more than three between 1989 and 2011. In parallel, these same multinational firms have destroyed a striking share of manufacturing jobs in the United States: of 19 million manufacturing jobs in 1980, only 11 million are left.[4] There is more than a simple correlation between these two movements. The destruction

---

[3] See www.globaljustice.org.uk/sites/default/files/files/resources/controlling_corporations_briefing.pdf.

[4] See www.bea.gov/scb/pdf/2013/11%20November/1113_mnc
.pdf and https://piie.com/blogs/trade-investment-policy-watch/
questionable-rationale-behind-washingtons-antitrade-rhetoric.

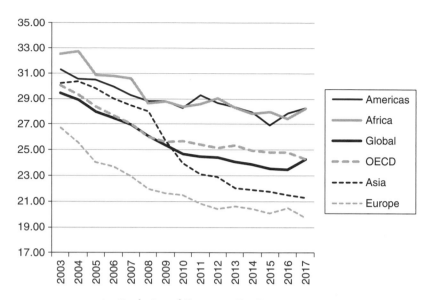

FIGURE 6.1 Evolution of Corporate Tax Rates, 2003–2017
Source: https://home.kpmg.com/xx/en/home/services/tax/tax-tools-and-resources/tax-rates-online/corporate-tax-rates-table.html.

of manufacturing jobs in rich countries and their transfer to parts of the world where labor is cheaper has been, over that period, one of the important factors generating an increase in profits for multi-national firms. Another explanatory mechanism for the increase in profits has been the striking decrease over the period of corporate tax rates, and this happened in all regions of the world, as illustrated in Figure 6.1 (which shows statutory tax rates, whereas actual taxes paid are even lower due to many special exemptions and loopholes).

Barkai (2017), relying on a model of monopolistic competition of the US economy, estimates that the growing concentration of the corporate sector has increased the firms' market power and their pure monopoly profits, while both the labor share and the capital share in value added decreased over the same period (Figure 6.2). This means that the market rate of return on capital actually went down during that period, and it brings an interesting variation to Piketty's theory

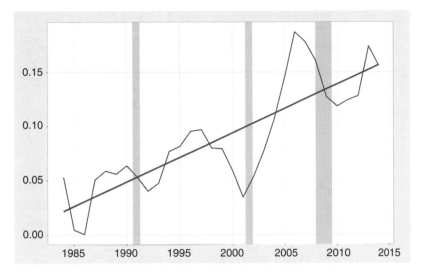

FIGURE 6.2 Pure Profit Share in the US Non-Financial Corporate Sector 1984–2014
Source: Barkai (2017).

of a stable rate of return and an increasing capital share – it is diffi-cult to separate the pure profit from the return on capital in the data.

The increasing wealth of multinational corporations and their rapid transnational projection have made them more powerful than ever. One of the consequences of the power and mobility of these corporations has been their capacity to select the legal jurisdictions that are the most favorable to their interests ("forum shopping"). Another important consequence, reflected in Figure 6.1, has been a compe-tition between countries to offer the most attractive tax conditions and deregulated labor markets for multinational corporations. This "tax and social dumping" has combined with the mechanism of off-shore tax havens to allow multinational corporations to reduce tax responsibility, or even dodge it altogether, on an unprecedented scale.

These evolutions have had an impact with regard to wealth appropriation. Multinational corporations have undeniably created significant wealth over the past forty years, but the largest share of that wealth has been transformed into profits rather than labor

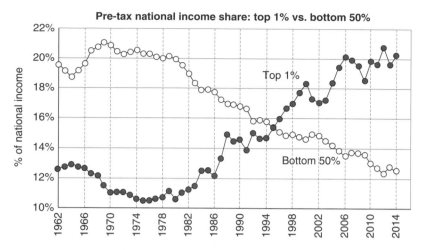

FIGURE 6.3 The Rise of the Super-Rich in the United States
Source: Piketty et al. (2016, appendix table II-B1).

remuneration or collective investments through taxes. Hence, it is fair to say that these evolutions have contributed to the significant increase in inequalities within countries, particularly in the Western world, that is by now well documented. As Figure 6.3 clearly indicates, increasing inequalities have led to the squeezing of the middle classes and the singular rising wealth of the (already) super-rich. While this phenomenon has been particularly strong in the United States, it can also be documented in the case of other countries (Piketty and Zucman 2014, Alvaredo et al. 2018).

These evolutions translate into direct threats to democracy. In 1911, the US Supreme Court Justice Louis D. Brandeis was already warning that "we can have democracy in this country, or we can have great wealth concentrated in the hands of a few, but we can't have both." The Gilded Age was a period in the United States also marked by wealth concentration and rising inequalities. Separation and balance of power, the existence of checks and balances that can weigh on dominant power nodes, are necessary conditions, we know, for the proper functioning of democracies (Dahl 2006). The extreme concentration of capital and wealth in contemporary corporations and the associated rise of the super-rich foster consequential democratic imbalances. In the twenty-first century, this applies well beyond the United States and can be documented in different parts of the world.

A first strong imbalance is created through the direct and significant political influence associated with large-scale financing of political campaigns and lobbying. In 2017 total spending on lobbying in the USA was around $3.36 billion, a 140 percent increase in less than twenty years.[5] This strong presence and influence of lobbying is also pervasive in other parts of the world – including in the European Union, where registration and declaration rules are less stringent than in the USA, making lobbying less easy to measure. And if lobbying was not enough, political contributions and campaign financing have also increased significantly over the last twenty years. This is leading to a situation where many would strongly argue that democratic politics have been captured and an oligarchic rule is coming to impose itself. The oligarchy, in this case, is a mix of big corporations and a small number of super-rich individuals, the two being often connected. In May 2017, Donald Trump decided to pull his country out of the COP21 Paris Agreement on climate change. A few weeks before this decision, twenty-two Republican senators had sent him a letter urging him to do so. As it turns out, those twenty-two senators received huge financial contributions during the last political campaigns from the oil, gas, and coal industries.[6] Hence, the link between concentrated wealth and undue political influence leading to a distortion of democracy can be quite direct and consequential. The broad question of the role of money in politics will be examined further in Chapter 8.

Corporations can have a more indirect but arguably still far-reaching impact. The exercise of corporate social responsibility (CSR) can be reinterpreted as a form of political intervention. Corporations are making consequential political decisions as they compensate

[5] See www.opensecrets.org/lobby/.
[6] See www.theguardian.com/us-news/2017/jun/01/republican-senators-paris-climate-deal-energy-donations.

for "failed states," act through delegation from disengaging states, or become increasingly involved in transnational multi-stakeholder rule-making. The aim behind CSR is in general a positive one, associated with the production of collective goods. CSR, however, just like philanthropy or paternalism before it, is associated with voluntarism, partiality, corporate discretion, and hence subjective involvement in certain causes and with certain groups and not others. This, undeniably, makes it impossible for CSR to deploy viable structural solutions for contemporary common-good challenges.

There is an even more subtle way in which the corporate world comes to distort democratic politics – through the financing of a vast array of think tanks and research institutes that organize for ideological influence and champion policy templates that tend to favor corporate interests. Climate change denial is again an interesting example here. Its ideological and political prevalence in the United States reflects more than direct campaign financing. We now know that it follows from more than thirty years of corporate financing of a dense network of think tanks pushing that agenda in extremely active ways (Jacques et al. 2008; Collomb 2014).

This wealth, power, and influence imbalance between corporations and most other actors (including states and politicians) in the political arena potentially has, we know, worrying consequences for our democracies. The rise of authoritarian governments and the temptation of populism and calls to erect walls and barriers between nations, communities, or individuals have to be understood at least in part in that context. Inequalities have become increasingly structural – curtailing opportunities for many and curbing intergenerational mobility. At the individual level, this may translate into a sense of alienation, anger, and violence, if not despair, that triggers a turn to populist policies and promises. The wealth and strength of contemporary corporations also translates into significant bargaining power in relation to labor. Corporations are, in themselves, among the least democratic institutions of our world – in fact they tend to function very much like autocracies. Corporations are characterized by strong internal inequalities which materialize in terms of remuneration, resources, power, and authority. And a very large majority of members of the corporation have no involvement whatsoever in decision-making and governance. Maybe it is not so surprising, in those conditions, that a large share of the Millennial generation does not project itself into a corporate future!

What can be done to address this challenge? Wealth and power imbalances, when they become too significant, represent a democratic threat and may even endanger the longer-term sustainability of capitalist arrangements. The above analysis suggests at least three courses of action.

First, we should demand complete transparency when it comes to the corporate financing of political campaigns and lobbying, but also influence activities through think tanks and research institutes. Transparency, however, is not enough. We need to set clear limits to the amounts that corporations or wealthy individuals can legally spend on political influence-building. More on this issue is coming up in Chapter 8.

Second, we need to impose fiscal responsibility. Corporations have to take on their proper share in the financing of uphill and downhill collective costs and externalities. The fight for fiscal responsibility will have to take different forms but it calls, in any case, for tight international collaboration and cooperation. The struggle against tax havens that has made significant progress over the past years should accelerate. Corporate tax rates need to be harmonized and set at levels that will allow for the deployment of adequate security and welfare provisions for members of those concerned territorial communities. Reliance on CSR will never be enough to align corporations with their real levels of responsibility when it comes to collective costs and externalities.

Third, encouraging the internal democratization of corporations and management forms can be helpful here as well. This goes beyond the redefinition of governance rules and guidelines already proposed in the previous section. It also implies the transformation of these ideological and cultural templates that frame the education and socialization of future corporate women and men, in particular managers. Managerial philosophies and instruments that foster participation, flat organization, inclusiveness, collaboration, and care should be valued, taught, and championed. We should in parallel come to question and recognize alienating modes of management for what they are – including in what is hailed today as the innovative, digital economy.

MARKETIZATION AND FINANCIALIZATION: UNEXPECTED BEDFELLOWS

The liberal project, with its roots in the Enlightenment, identified the market economy as an important mechanism of wealth creation and individual liberation. In contrast to various forms of corporatism – including the corporation, according to Adam Smith – the "free market" would allow for an efficient allocation of resources and for a matching of demand and supply with minimal distortion. The competition mechanism was the key process through which the fair(est) prices emerged.

The liberal tradition in economics sees the market and market economies as the "natural" state for humanity, a state that has been impeded, frustrated, or even blocked in different periods and parts of the world (Hayek 1944). Other thinkers, however, such as Karl Polanyi in his landmark 1944 book *The Great Transformation*, have underscored the socially constructed nature (through time) of the market economy as an increasingly powerful and dominant form of human organization. In the end, who is right in this debate is not so important. Of significance, however, is the trend that has seen the rapid progress of "marketization" in our contemporary world since the late 1970s. By "marketization" here one should understand both the belief and conviction that markets are of superior efficiency for the allocation of goods and resources and the reform and policy practices associated with this, including macroeconomic stabilization, privatization, deregulation, and liberalization of foreign trade.

The progress of marketization over that period has seen an increasing number of countries transforming themselves into market economies or expanding the role and place of market logics in the organization of their economies. Even more spectacular, though, has been the domain expansion of marketization. Market logics have reached spheres of human and social life that had traditionally been structured and valued through very different mechanisms: health, education, sports, and even arts, culture, politics, religion, or intimate relationships. The market has become a dominant mantra and a magic wand across many boundaries.

Three main issues need to be underscored here. First, markets undeniably can be, and have historically been, effective mechanisms of allocation and wealth creation. But one important condition for the "undistorted" and "free" functioning of markets is that they be characterized by open and fair competition, where no single actor is able to dictate or control market conditions. The transformation of contemporary capitalism described above runs against this condition. In particular the financial capital aggregation associated with corporatization on a large scale is in principle quite in contradiction to effective mechanisms of free-market allocation. In our contemporary period, many markets have moved toward oligopolistic equilibria, and in some cases those oligopolies are structured at the international level. In conditions of oligopolistic equilibrium, the virtuous role of market dynamics becomes much less obvious. The power of certain actors allows them to tilt market conditions in their favor and creates space for the development of rent-seeking behaviors. In such a context, the "magic of the market" is likely to be no more than an incantation, strongly decoupled from the dynamics that are at work in reality. Second, even if and when market mechanisms function in a satisfactory manner with respect to competitive dynamics, and wealth is effectively produced, questions remain with respect to the distribution of the wealth thus created. The last 150 years of market economy show that the two issues of wealth production and wealth distribution are not miraculously connected, as the Adam Smith imagery of the "invisible hand" would lead some to argue. Wealth production through markets can, in other words, be associated with very unfair and undemocratic patterns of wealth distribution. Third, the progress and success of marketization begs the question of the "moral limits of markets" (Sandel 2013; Satz 2010). A market, after all, implies that the goods or services that are being exchanged are (and can be) commodified. The marketization of (nearly) everything hence would imply the commodification and the forcing of monetary valuation on (nearly) everything. The question we need to ask ourselves is whether, indeed, everything (including for example organs, bodies, children, relationships, culture, education, political influence ...) can be and should be turned into tradable goods with a monetary value.

As suggested above, a defining feature of contemporary capitalism is the surprising co-evolution of marketization and financialization trends – whereas in theory both could be seen as in partial contradiction (Krippner 2005; Palley 2013). The process of financialization has, itself, a number of dimensions. It refers, on the one hand, to the increasing role and place of financial markets in the economy in general, and to the increasing number of firms all around seeking funds on those markets. The logic is straightforward: as our economic and social activities are being transformed into commodities, financial markets take center stage as the main arenas in which the corporations producing those commodities are priced and traded. Financialization also refers, naturally, to the increasing role played by financial indicators in the decision-making process of many economic actors, including but also well beyond corporations, sometimes to the exclusion of other kinds of indicators. As already indicated, this importance of financial indicators has reached spheres of human and social life that had very different reference frames before, such as personal care. Financialization also occurs through the increasing clout of finance as an industry and as a professional field, and the great success with which this industry has managed to subjugate all forms of constraints – institutional, political, even ethical – to the seamless globalization and expansion of its activities.

Financialization also translates in numbers – stunning numbers that reflect capital aggregation on an unprecedented scale and significantly at odds with the concurrent calls for "free-market" dynamics. In 1980, the market capitalization of listed domestic companies in Europe was about 8 percent of GDP. This number soared to 105 percent in 1999, and has fluctuated between 40 percent and 90 percent since 2002.[7] In 1997, the total value of securitization (i.e. assets composed of various debts) in Europe was 47 billion euros. By 2008, it had reached 2,200 billion euros.[8] If we turn now to the global derivatives market (most of which are exchanged privately "over the counter"), the figures are even more staggering. From a global value in 1998 of 72 trillion dollars, this market shot up to close to 550 trillion dollars in 2016.[9]

Since the crisis of 2007, we know that the intense and rapid financialization of our economies and societies has a pervasive speculative dimension. A fair share of the value that had been created on financial markets before 2007 vanished as the crisis unfolded. The particular form of speculative financialization characteristic of contemporary capitalism justifies qualifications of "casino capitalism" (Sinn 2010). It has inexorably created significant destabilizing pressures on our world economies but also societies and polities.

How can we address these challenges? Paradoxically perhaps, in view of the incantatory dimension of contemporary marketization, it is urgent to reinject truly competitive dynamics in the organization of our economies. There are a number of possible and complementary paths for that. First, working in the context of anti-trust

[7] Source: www.indexmundi.com/facts/european-union/market-capitalization-of-listed-companies.

[8] Source: http://eur-lex.europa.eu/legal-content/EN/TXT/PDF/?uri=CELEX:52015SC0185&from=EN.

[9] Source: www.bis.org/statistics/derstats.htm. These figures represent the "notional value," which includes double-counting of the underlying assets. The total market value of the underlying assets was around 20 trillion dollars in 2016.

regulatory communities to redefine concentration thresholds could have a very powerful and structural impact. Second, we need to strongly incentivize the development of new firms and foster the intensification of start-up ecologies, particularly in those industries that have been dominated for too long by large oligopolies, such as energy systems, and by over-protective property rights, such as the pharmaceutical industry. The institutional incentives that we need to set up should not only foster the creation of start-ups but should also discourage, beyond certain levels, dynamics of integration and capital concentration.

When it comes to the invasive growth of marketization and market logics, we should effectively restart a public debate on the limits and morally acceptable boundaries of the market. Beyond the proper scientific assessment of the efficiency of market solutions in different areas, which is overdue, national and transnational political actors have the responsibility to foster democratic debates and resolutions with a view to containing market logics and putting limits on their expansion. In order to revive this type of political debate, we need to encourage the development of alternative solutions and their carriers, from within communities, NGOs, universities, research institutes, and the community of think tanks and policy influencers. Among the latter group, champions of free-market solutions have been particularly active and effective channels of diffusion and institutionalization over the last thirty years or so. It is urgent to encourage the development of challenger ideas (Held 2004). While we objectively moved, since the fall of the Berlin Wall, toward the dominance of an intolerant paradigm (Babb 2012), we need to reinvent a culture of debate and dissonance and to revive a competitive ecology of ideas. This should start at the heart of socialization institutions: we need to rethink the training of future elites and experts, particularly within economics departments and business, law, and government schools.

Finally, we need to work in parallel on the problematic sides of contemporary financialization. A well-functioning capitalism naturally needs finance. But finance should be brought back to where it belongs – at the service of economic development and ultimately human prosperity. There are many paths to follow if we want to go in that direction. Some propositions have already been outlined in the above two sections, since an important feature of contemporary finance is its corporatization. We also urgently need to make financial regulation work at the transnational level. Global finance is a common good that needs control. Stricter regulation might have to come with the reinvention and adaptation to our times of old solutions – Glass Steagall,[10] for example, or even partial or complete nationalization of some key actors. In parallel, it is urgent to foster the development and growth of alternative forms of finance, i.e. organizations and arrangements with a more prudential, cooperative, and community-based focus and a strong engagement in favor of a sustainable and progressive economy and society.

---

[10] In 1933, the Glass-Steagall Act separated commercial and investment banks, in order to protect household savings from speculation.

7 From the Welfare State to the Emancipating State

In *The Great Transformation* (1944), Karl Polanyi argues that the market economy is not well equipped to deal with three goods which are not ordinary commodities because they cannot be produced by commercial companies: land, labor, and money. It is indeed well accepted that money needs state guarantee to attract sufficient trust and ward off speculation – bitcoin and alternative local currencies try to prove this wrong, and might prove it right. The case of land also relates to environmental issues more broadly, and indeed in this domain, market failures are widespread and involve not just pollution but also externalities in the choice of land use and habitat (for instance, urban real estate is vulnerable to spontaneous segregation patterns). The case of labor is central in Polanyi's book, which is very much about the birth of proto-welfare states in the wake of the Industrial Revolution. Labor is not a commercial good, because people need to live and cannot simply disappear when they cease to be profitable. The market does not spontaneously guarantee survival and economic security for any commodity, and if labor is made a commodity, as happens in capitalism, the survival and security of *people* is therefore jeopardized. The wild fluctuations of markets disrupt lives repeatedly, under multiple shocks, and nowadays globalization and technological change are accelerating the movements, as analyzed in Chapter 2.

Polanyi argues that for the market economy to be compatible with security for the population, it needs to be "embedded" in social mechanisms of insurance and solidarity which come to the rescue when market incomes fail some parts of the population. He provides an impressive description of the Industrial Revolution as a movement of *disembedding* – the market economy freeing itself from the shackles of traditional communities – which at the same time unleashed formidable economic dynamism and threw many vulnerable households into disruptive transitions. Many attempts to provide social assistance to poor households were made in the nineteenth century, which foreshadowed later developments in the modern post-Second World War welfare states – in particular with similar hesitations about conditional and unconditional income support.

IPSP (2018a, chapter 1) draws a parallel with the deregulation movement of the late twentieth century, which can similarly be viewed as a disembedding of the globalized market system from the constraints of national Keynesian institutions and the tax obligations they carried for the sake of macroeconomic management and social solidarity. Successful businesses and the super-rich today are, with very few exceptions, globalized agents. Even when they draw their main source of wealth from national privileges (like Carlos Slim in the Mexican monopolistic system, or Russian oligarchs in the Kremlin orbit), their investment horizons and consumption lifestyle go well beyond national borders and certainly include exotic tax havens.

The obvious conclusion at this juncture is that a new re-embedding of the market system into institutions of social solidarity is needed. An obvious option is to draw from the Keynesian toolkit again, since it was quite successful in the three decades following the Second World War, and to transpose it to the new globalized setting: a world government with global taxes and global income support systems, allowing transfers from growing regions to stagnating regions, from thriving populations to struggling ones, would go a long way toward addressing the current rifts in social cohesion between and within countries. The calls for a global or at least regional Tobin tax on financial transactions, for tax coordination across countries, for the suppression of tax havens, or for a global capital tax (Piketty 2014) all draw their inspiration from this reasoning.

It would indeed be great to make progress in that direction, but this line of reasoning suffers from three limitations. First, building a world government is not in the air these days, and the current difficulties of Europe do not bode well for the political prospects of this ideal in the short or medium term. The trend is now at least as much to split countries into autonomous regions. Second, given this observed need for local autonomy in political and economic management, centralization may become counterproductive beyond a certain scale. Therefore, it is debatable whether world institutions should take on a big burden, and there may be a real danger that they could take on too much and do more harm than good. Third, the Keynesian worldview was rather limited as regards social progress. It was essentially a pragmatic approach to the management of capitalism, without much ambition as far as human development was concerned. Somehow, we now need to add John Rawls' and Amartya Sen's ideas to John Maynard Keynes', and this may call for a more structural reform of capitalism, as already argued in the previous chapter.

Precisely, this chapter builds on the previous one to explore how a new re-embedding of the market system in social solidarity institutions can be conceived for the twenty-first century. Can a new welfare state be invented with the ambition of achieving substantial social progress?

THE WELFARE STATE UNDER PRESSURE

Over the past 150 years, national welfare state interventions have played an increasing role in the provision of collective solidarity. Even though ancient forms of welfare interventions existed in the history of human societies, the context has radically changed since the middle of the nineteenth century. The development of capitalism (which replaced feudal, religious, or agro-pastoral traditional forms of appropriation and solidarity provisions), the Industrial Revolution (which generalized mechanized production modes and created new types of vulnerable workers and strong rewards for individual skills), and the emergence of nation-states (which introduced a new layer of authority and of collective belonging) created the basis for the development of national welfare state interventions to alleviate poverty

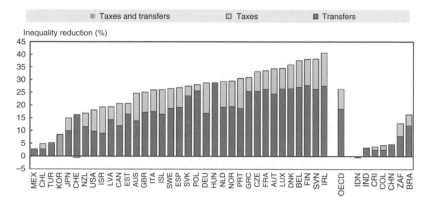

FIGURE 7.1 Inequality Reduction by Taxes and Transfers 2013–2014
Source: OECD (2017, fig. 12).

and reduce social inequalities. The widespread development of welfare states, from the European core to almost all developing countries (though with very significant variations), is a key feature of capitalist development in the twentieth century.

Among the important contributions of the welfare state is the reduction of inequality. Altogether, taxes and transfers substantially reduce the inequalities that market incomes generate. As Figure 7.1 shows, inequalities as measured by the Gini coefficient would be much higher, almost twice as large in some countries (Ireland, Finland, Belgium), without government redistribution. In the US, government redistribution is less effective and cuts only about a fifth of inequalities.

Why is the welfare state now under pressure, or even in crisis as often alleged in the media? Some of the challenges are merely political or even ideological. The conservative wave which, after Reagan, argued that "government is the problem, not the solution" developed a program aimed at rolling back welfare provisions and public services without any objective reason but with abhorrent spiteful feelings toward the "welfare queens," with racial undertones. It is worth recalling that, as a matter of fact, government did not shrink that much under Reagan, and quite to the contrary, defense expenditures

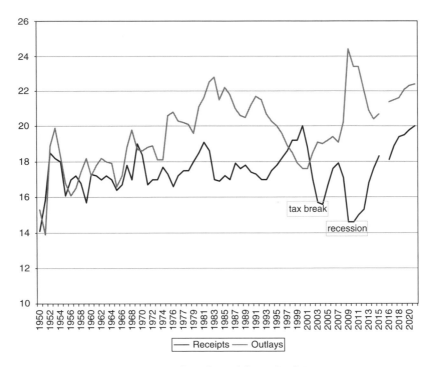

FIGURE 7.2 Receipts and Outlays of the Federal Government as a
Percentage of GDP, USA 1950–2015 and Forecast for 2016–2021
Source: https://obamawhitehouse.archives.gov/sites/default/files/omb/
budget/fy2017/assets/hist01z3.xls.

went through the ceiling. Much more impactful was G.W. Bush's
tax break (also accompanied by defense expenditures during the Iraq
war), as can be seen in Figure 7.2. For the record, the figure includes
forecasts by the Obama administration for the coming years, which
does not take into account the latest Trump tax reform.

This figure should lay to rest the talk about governments
losing their revenue capacities and rolling back state interventions.
Figure 7.3 shows that there is no downward trend on public social
spending in the OECD countries, even if some important fluctuations
have occurred, in particular in the 1990s.[1]

---

[1] In Greece, Spain, Italy, and Portugal, social public spending has been stalled or
slightly reduced in per capita terms under the recent austerity policies, but has
increased as a percentage of GDP due to the recession reinforced by austerity itself.

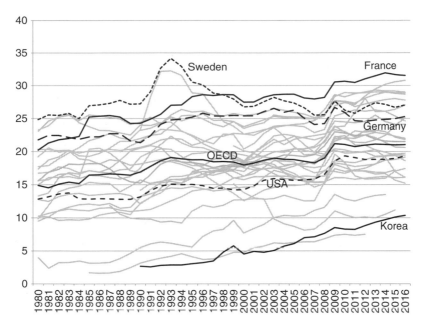

FIGURE 7.3 Public Social Expenditure in the OECD as a Percentage of GDP, 1980–2016
Source: OECD.Stat.

Another widespread misconception related to Reagan's "government is the problem" mantra also undermines support for the welfare state. This is the idea that only the private sector creates value whereas the government merely moves resources around, taking from some and giving to others, without creating anything. In fact, through its provision of infrastructures and services, its insurance support to risk-takers, the government is a catalyst for economic activities and most government expenditures have an investment flavor, which is unfortunately not recognized as such in national accounts. Some of these so-called expenditures are extremely profitable, as famously argued by James Heckman about early childhood education: "Those seeking to reduce deficits and strengthen the economy should make significant investments in early childhood education."[2] There is today a clear consensus that early childhood education and care, if of good quality, brings a wide range of benefits, including better child wellbeing and learning outcomes, more equitable outcomes and reduction of poverty, increased intergenerational social mobility, higher female labor market participation and gender equality, and better social and economic development for society at large. Very high benefits can also be obtained with investments in higher education. In 2015, the World Bank showed that in the world in general and Africa in particular, rates of return for higher education were becoming higher than those for primary or secondary education. The issue is not choosing one sector over another, but striking the right balance between investments in various education levels, notably given the strong challenges posed by the global knowledge economy.[3]

REAL CHALLENGES

But there are real challenges for the welfare state in the twenty-first century. Here is a list of the main issues already playing out or coming up in the next decades.

First, as already shown in Chapters 2 (Figure 2.9) and 6 (Figure 6.1), corporate tax rates have been declining. The stability of federal government receipts in the US, as shown in Figure 7.2, hides a scissors movement by which a steady decline in the effective corporate tax rate has been replaced by a growing portion of receipts coming from payroll tax. Piketty (2014) shows that the reduction in top tax rates in the US went hand-in-hand with the explosion of income inequality and wealth concentration witnessed over the past thirty years. Globalization is putting pressure on the taxation of mobile factors, capital and highly skilled labor, which undermines the capacity of the government to curb inequalities. Indeed, compensating for the reduced corporate and top income taxes with higher

---

[2] See https://heckmanequation.org/resource/invest-in-early-childhood-development-reduce-deficits-strengthen-the-economy/.

[3] See IPSP (2018c, chapter 19) and Salmi (2017).

levels of income taxes on lower revenues and greater reliance on value-added taxes curbs the inequality-reducing effectiveness of taxes and transfers. Shifting the tax burden from capital to labor is also unwise at a time of structural unemployment (as in some European countries) and at the onset of an automation wave that will displace many jobs.

This first challenge is about receipts. There are important challenges also on the outlays side. One comes from ageing, which increases the burden of the dependent on the active workers, adding further pressure to increase taxes on incomes. This challenge can be addressed by investing massively in order to raise labor productivity and to generate capital income, provided the government makes sure to control or collect this capital income via a mandatory system of contributory pensions or the build-up of a sovereign fund. The automation wave would be welcome in this context, if one could make sure that the working-age labor force could find good productive jobs and would not massively end up in low-productivity service jobs.

Another way to address the ageing challenge is to invite foreign young workers from countries with an excess of labor force. A youth bulge in Africa coinciding with an ageing population in Europe seems like an almost ideal solution to the problem. The difficulty is that if the linkage takes the form of migrations of workers and their families, rapidly increasing heterogeneity in European societies will further inflate xenophobic and racist tendencies. It would also undermine support for the welfare state. Indeed, as reflected in IPSP (2018a, chapter 2, and 2018c, chapter 20), solidarity is a cornerstone value of human societies and this sense of solidarity – or of collective responsibility toward welfare – is critically related to a sense of belonging and identity. This interaction between welfare, solidarity, and belonging in human societies is a key aspect which helps explain why solidarity mechanisms are less robust in heterogeneous societies with loose links between diverse populations. Perceptions of growing diversity in some countries may undermine the solidarity ethos and erode popular support for the welfare state.

Yet another way of making use of the coincidence of workers in developing countries and pensioners in rich countries is to make the massive investment mentioned earlier to create jobs in the developing countries themselves. But many of these countries have difficulties guaranteeing stability and security for investments – actually, a youth bulge is also a recipe for political unrest and vulnerability to terrorist enrollment. And this way of exploiting transnational capitalism to solve social issues in the rich countries may not seem appealing to developing countries eager to reach economic independence.

Besides ageing, health expenditures also generate a serious challenge. This is partly related to ageing, since a growing number of dependent elderly people will need assistance for more years than in previous times. But such assistance largely takes the form of services which are not that costly. More challenging is the transformation in health innovation, which now produces new devices and new drugs which make it possible to explore the human body in extremely detailed ways and design very personalized treatments, but at a cost that cannot be supported for the whole population. The time is gone of simple antibiotics and X-ray and echography devices that can be made accessible to everyone. New scanners cost millions of dollars and new drugs often cost hundreds of thousands of dollars per year of treatment. We may also be on the verge of a new wave of bacterial infections resisting antibiotic treatment and needing more costly interventions. The key issue for the welfare state is that, now, the question of choosing which procedures and treatments are covered and which are not is much more painful than it used to be, because many patients will end up knowing about possible treatments that will not be covered even though they might save them. The problem is compounded by the concentration of the pharmaceutical industry, which enables it to practice opaque pricing and argue that astronomical mark-ups are justified by its large R&D costs – which cannot be true given that this industry is extremely profitable.

To address this challenge, one should probably combine an aggressive stance on restoring competition in the pharmaceutical

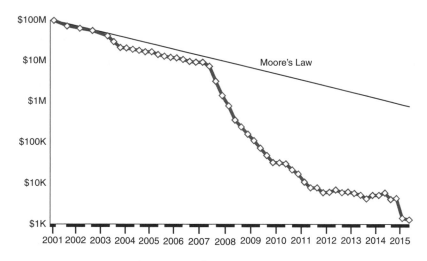

FIGURE 7.4 Declining Cost of DNA Sequencing
Source: NIH.

industry, rewarding medical innovation in other ways than with large
and arbitrary mark-ups,[4] setting up a single-payer system better able
to negotiate prices, and encouraging cost-saving innovations. Many
costly procedures have seen their costs dwindle, which is promising.
For instance, DNA sequencing of the human genome has seen its
cost decline from millions of dollars to less than $1,000, much more
quickly than Moore's law (which was proposed for the capacity of
computing), as illustrated in Figure 7.4.

The automation wave will challenge both the receipts side and
the outlays side of public finances. Even if, as appears most likely, it
will not make labor disappear but will only transform the composition of jobs, the transition may be hard if the pace of job dislocations
is quick. In the coming decades, we may face a growing number of

---

[4] There are interesting initiatives seeking to assess the global health impact of
medical innovations and design a reward scheme for innovators that would
bypass the patent system and make it possible to incentivize innovation toward
medical needs (rather than market demand) and to enable the quick diffusion
by imitation of new inventions. See http://global-health-impact.org/ and http://
healthimpactfund.org/.

middle-aged workers whose skills have become suddenly obsolete and whose prospects of finding a decent job before their retirement age are scant. This will both dampen tax revenues and increase income support expenditures. This is where determined political action, through corporation reform and through government incentives, to direct the pace and orientation of automation toward a smoother and more worker-friendly process, as argued for in Chapters 2 and 6, is important. But one must also recognize the need for the development of public or subsidized lifelong education systems helping workers navigate a new era in which it is no longer standard to keep the same type of job throughout a full career.

A final challenge, these days, comes from the fact that public debt has been seriously inflated by the financial crisis (Figure 7.5), and that important economies such as those of the G7 countries would find it difficult to shoulder a similar shock in the near term. Unfortunately, it is not unlikely that financial instability will continue, as the regulations set in place after the last crisis are deemed insufficient by experts and are being rolled back in the US.

An important clarification that must be made about the welfare state is that differences in welfare provisions across countries are less deep than they seem. In countries with a smaller expanse of public provision, households must still spend on housing, education, health care, and pensions. According to the OECD, which has been carefully monitoring this issue over the past decade, "when private spending and tax systems are included, total spending differences diminish across countries." Figure 7.6 shows that a most spectacular readjustment affects the USA, which jumps from a low public-expenditure rank to the second highest total-expenditure rank. The key difference between public and private spending lies much less in the amount than in the distribution of resources and freedom for citizens. Leaving essential expenditures to the private sphere worsens inequalities. The discussion should thus focus less on the (over)size of the welfare state than on the efficiency of welfare systems as such in the global age.

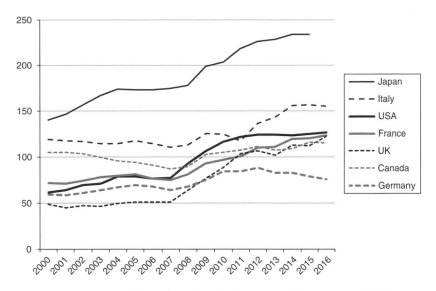

FIGURE 7.5 Public Debt in the G7 Countries, in Percentage of GDP
Source: OECD.Stat.

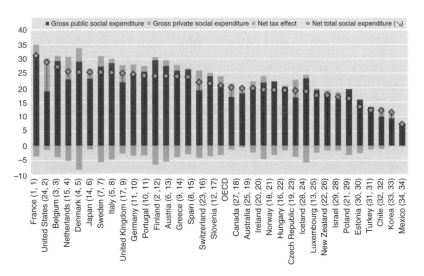

FIGURE 7.6 Total Net Spending in the OECD as a Percentage of
GDP, 2013
Source: OECD (2016, fig. 4).

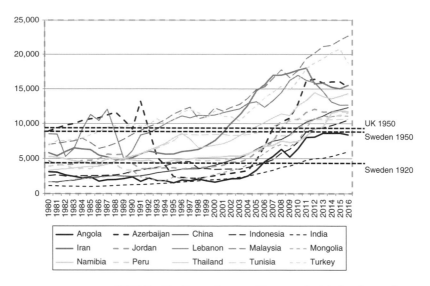

FIGURE 7.7 GDP Per Capita, 1960–2011 Compared with Sweden and UK at Onset of Welfare Reforms
Source: Maddison Project.

IS WELFARE ONLY FOR THE RICH?

Another widespread misconception is that only the richest economies can afford an ambitious welfare state. In fact, England, Germany, France, Sweden, and the US scaled up their welfare state interventions with levels of GDP per capita that were similar to current levels reached by emerging countries, as illustrated in Figure 7.7. Indonesia and China are now more developed than America was in 1935 when it passed the Social Security Act, or even than Britain was in 1948, when it started its monumental National Health Service (NHS). The Scandinavian countries built key components of their welfare states before the Second World War (Sweden introduced its universal pension system in 1913), at an even lower level of economic development, and their development process was enhanced, not hindered, by a better-educated and more productive workforce and an efficient wage formation system through centralized collective bargaining.

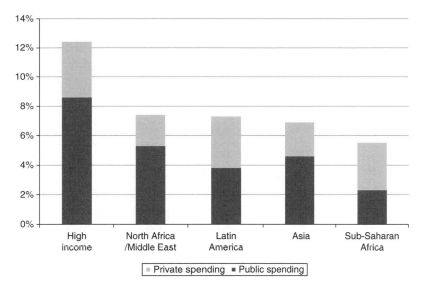

FIGURE 7.8 Public and Private Spending on Health (Percentage of GDP), 2015
Source: World Bank.

Indeed, the recent period has seen a rapid increase in welfare state interventions in developing countries, though still far below the levels observed in high-income countries (see Figures 7.8 and 7.9).

Take the example of Asia. In 2011, the Indonesian parliament passed a law setting up health insurance for all of the country – the largest single-payer system in the world. The same law also committed the government to extending pensions, death benefits, and worker-accident insurance to the whole nation. In the Philippines, the government-owned health insurer, PhilHealth, covers most of the population. Thailand achieved universal health care in 2001 and introduced pensions for the informal sector a decade later. India expanded its job-guarantee program to every rural district in 2008, offering up to 100 days of minimum wage work a year to every rural household applying for it. In 2008, Korea introduced an earned-income tax credit, a universal basic pension, and an insurance scheme providing long-term care for the elderly. China's rural health

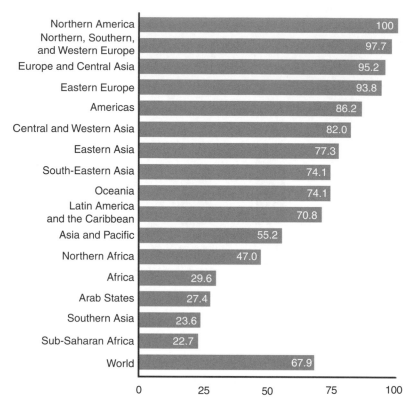

FIGURE 7.9 Population above Pensionable Age Receiving a Pension (Percentage)
Source: ILO (2017, fig. 4.3).

insurance scheme, which in 2003 covered 3 percent of the eligible population, has now almost achieved full coverage, according to official statistics. India has also extended a modest formula of health insurance to hundreds of millions of uninsured people.

These efforts intend to counter the growing dissatisfaction of large segments of the population in transition economies that experienced a surge in economic growth. As reported in IPSP (2018a, chapter 8):

> life satisfaction in China actually declined, on average, in the last decades, and this was accompanied by increases in suicide rates and incidence of mental illness (Graham et al. 2015). Survey

responses by income categories taken in 1990 and 2007 show that life satisfaction declined in the bottom two income categories, but increased in the top income category (Easterlin et al. 2012).

This led Chinese authorities to increase public social spending by 50 percent between 2007 and 2012, even though the 2012 level (9 percent of GDP) was still well below the OECD average and that of Korea (11 percent). Countries such as Chile, Mexico, and Turkey spend less than 15 percent of GDP on social support. Although relatively low in international comparisons, over the past twenty-five years public social expenditures as a percentage of GDP doubled in Mexico and Turkey.

Latin America has a much longer tradition of social security schemes and welfare states interventions. In pioneering countries (Argentina, Brazil, Chile, Uruguay, and Cuba), the main social security schemes were in place before the Second World War and grew following the pace of industrialization and economic growth (with the notable exception of Cuba, which followed a radical track after the 1960s). These pioneer countries plus Costa Rica had achieved high levels of health coverage by 1980, with over 60 percent of the population covered (see Huber and Bogliaccini, 2010). In the following twenty years, however, welfare states in Latin America underwent drastic reforms and transformations in the context of large-scale privatization and repeated fiscal crises. The ascent to power of left-of-center governments, in the first decade of the twenty-first century, reinforced comprehensive and equity-oriented social policy. A few successful programs prove that costs do not have to be too high. For example, Bolsa Familia in Brazil costs less than 0.5 percent of GDP and reaches 26 percent of the population, while Progresa-Oportunidades in Mexico costs 0.4 percent of GDP and reaches 5 million households (European Commission 2010).

In Africa, many southern countries already have social pension systems, and many sub-Saharan countries have made remarkable progress toward the institutionalization of social protection: Burkina

Faso, Ghana, Kenya, Mozambique, Rwanda, Sierra Leone, and Uganda, among others, have adopted or are in the process of adopting social protection strategies as part of building comprehensive social protection systems. Countries such as Benin, Burkina, Côte d'Ivoire, Gabon, Mali, Senegal, and Tanzania have been reforming their social protection mechanisms to implement universal health coverage, taking inspiration from the leading examples of Ghana and Rwanda. Many of the successful programs (e.g. Ghana's National Health Insurance Scheme, Rwanda's Vision 2020 Umurenge Program, Lesotho's Old Age Pension) appear very effective in reaching the poorest, which in itself is quite an achievement, especially without producing significant distortions or disincentives (European Commission 2010). There is much to learn for other continents from these successful and fiscally sustainable "home-grown" welfare state interventions in Africa.

RETHINKING THE WELFARE STATE

In the history of capitalism, three conceptions of welfare state, identified in Esping-Andersen's (1990) pioneering work, provide a very useful way of understanding the multiple and complex variations of welfare institutions in developed and developing countries.

The first conception can be called the "Anglo-Saxon," even if neither the US nor the UK offers a pure illustration of it. It combines a freewheeling shareholder economy with a minimal welfare state which restricts its interventions to income support targeting the poorest (minimum pension, minimum health care, food stamps). It leaves opt-out options and private supplements for the rich. This model has the advantage of being very lean in expenditures, and therefore amenable to few tax distortions of economic activity and an easily achieved fiscal balance. It is not promising in terms of social progress, however, because it is not effective in tackling the strong inequalities generated by the economy. It is vulnerable to a vicious circle, when the targeted interventions stigmatize the poor and increase social polarization, which undermines middle-class support for poverty relief, because the poor are then perceived as a burden on the hard-working population. This pushes for shrinking welfare support and further polarizes society in a downward spiral. This spiral is all the more likely in a society divided by ethnic differences correlated with social inequalities. In a way, one can say that Ronald Reagan's attack on the "welfare queens" started such a spiral in the US, at least as regards minimum income support, which is now, especially after Clinton's 1996 reform, much less generous than it used to be.

The second conception is the "corporatist," or Bismarckian. It involves a greater tax burden involving insurance for workers, financed by payroll contributions, with favorable treatment of insiders and very minimal direct government support of outsiders. This form has been dominant in parts of continental Europe, as well as in Latin America and some Asian countries, where the state emerged before society, making this form a natural option. This model, like the previous one, also divides society and is therefore unable to really close the gap between those who succeed on the labor market and those whose careers fail to start at an early age or meet an abrupt end in middle age due to layoffs. Given the growing complexity of the labor market, and the fact that careers will be less and less linear with the automation wave, this formula now seems unable to adapt to the new imperative to protect people rather than jobs.

The third formula is the "social-democratic" one, well established in Scandinavian countries. It is precisely built around the principle of protecting people, not jobs. It has three concrete pillars. First, universal services are extensive and strongly invest in the human capital of the population. Their universality, associated with efficient management of the government structures delivering them, attracts large-scale popular support for the system, and avoids stigmatizing the most disadvantaged members of the population. They also enhance gender equality in the workplace and in families thanks to extensive care services and gender-sensitive parental leave. Second, the economy is open and market discipline operates to select

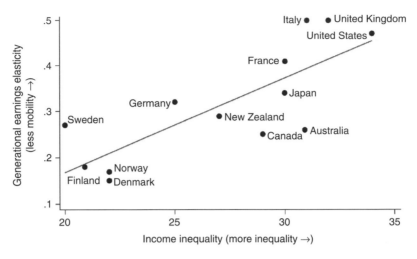

FIGURE 7.10 The Great Gatsby Curve: More Inequality Is Associated with Lower Social Mobility
Source: Corak (2013).

and promote the most productive businesses, without any special effort to protect jobs, since generous income and training support take care of helping workers transition to new jobs ("flexicurity"). Third, centralized bargaining involving state, business, and union representatives determines relatively equal and stable earnings, and wage moderation makes the economy profitable and competitive in the world market, while wage compression across the economy (in firms and between firms) incentivizes the adoption of recent technology and boosts productivity, forcing the laggards that cannot pay good wages out of the market. This model has an impressive coherence, and offers a remarkable blend of market competition and cooperative management. Over time, the achieved equality within a given generation enhances opportunities for the next generation and intergenerational mobility. These countries have greater social mobility than more unequal countries, as shown in Figure 7.10.

Of the three approaches, the social-democratic one is obviously the most promising for the twenty-first century, given its compatibility with open markets and rapid innovation, and its more substantial success in achieving social justice. It is even argued in IPSP (2018a, chapter 8) that the experience of the Scandinavian countries, which built their welfare state at an early stage in their development proves that equality, as achieved by such formula, is a good strategy for development. This contradicts the conventional wisdom that development needs to go through a phase of growing inequality before redistribution can take place. This point echoes Heckman's advocacy: strong investment in human capital is very productive, and therefore an unequal development path is actually a wasteful one, failing to tap the potential of its population.

The social-democratic model, however, is probably not the "end of history." First, it may not be easy to transplant it to countries where the centralized bargaining system would run against decentralized traditions and would suffer from a lack of representative organizations. But more importantly, it does not empower workers and citizens as much as one could hope for this century. None of the three welfare state formulas, arguably, can successfully address the inequalities in power and status that are typical of the capitalist economy. Quite to the contrary, they actually entrench them by making such inequalities compatible with substantial equality in resources. State protection itself runs the risk of being paternalistic, while centralized bargaining procedures can stifle local, "home-grown," or bottom-up social innovation.

Even if, in the social-democratic formula, individual workers and families do have much stronger bargaining positions in their workplace and on the labor market thanks to their human capital and the protection of the state, the fact remains that most of the key decisions are made over their heads, either in the centralized bargaining round, or by their employers. The social-democratic system is more a "grand bargain" between capital and labor than a transformation of capital providers and labor providers into real partners in every business, as envisioned in Chapter 6.

One can imagine a new form of welfare state that builds on the social-democratic formula but replaces the centralized bargaining pillar with a decentralized democratization of the economy, in particular through reform of the corporation and democratization of every business along the lines discussed in Chapter 6.

This new model of decentralized social democracy may be worth experimenting with. While the government retains its traditional function of providing public goods, services, and social insurance enabling private agents to be secure and take risks, it acquires the new role of guaranteeing and monitoring economic democracy through the involvement of stakeholders in all decision bodies which affect their interests substantially. The participatory forms of local democracy tested in Latin America and now widely imitated everywhere (see Chapter 8) also partake of the same idea that decisions should be taken under the control of those who are directly affected by them. Applying this idea to the economy, not just to local politics, would be the key principle of this fourth model of welfare state. This new type of social welfare would therefore replace the idea of the state providing "welfare" with the idea of the state "emancipating" people, given them new rights and capabilities, and enabling them to flourish by themselves.

THE EMANCIPATING STATE: FEATURES AND CHALLENGES

The proposed model would take place in a larger move to more deeply address the inequalities of the capitalist economy and toward a new form of democratic market economy, in which private property remains dominant but in which the typical capitalist inequalities of power and status would be contained. Like social democracy, this model would reduce the need for redistribution *after* market incomes have been formed by intervening *before* the market – through investing in human capital – and *in* the market – by improving the distribution of power in economic decisions by businesses and economic organizations. In particular, more democratic businesses tend to have much less unequal wage distributions than traditional firms. In this way, market incomes would be less unequal, and therefore less taxes and transfers would be needed, which would reduce the distortionary burden of income taxation on the economy.[5]

One positive feature of the traditional social-democratic formula is wage compression obtained through centralized bargaining. In a decentralized system, even if wage inequalities remain modest *within* (democratic) firms, they may widen *between* firms if there is no constraint on local decisions. There may then be a risk of one sector of the economy falling behind in terms of productivity and income. But centralization of collective bargaining is not really needed to ward off this threat. It is sufficient to implement a minimum wage policy to force all businesses to reach a minimum level of productivity.

The automation wave, in the proposed model, could be at least partly tackled through four mechanisms. First, workplace transformations would be more worker-friendly in companies taking account of stakeholder interests. This may slow the rise in labor productivity but be overall positive for the economy by smoothing the transition and therefore reducing its social costs. Second, income support and lifelong learning would help workers transition to new jobs. Third, a reduction in taxes on labor would make labor-saving innovations less attractive. Fourth, the development of externality-pricing through taxes and subsidies (on which more will be said below) would make firms at least partly internalize the social costs of their decisions.

Another development that appears sensitive from the standpoint of the new model is the expansion of the gig economy. The sharing economy offers low security and a range of degrees of dependence of contractors with respect to their platforms. A safety net for all (e.g. in the form of a basic income) would go some way toward avoiding the worst forms of exploitation in this sector, but ideally, one would also want to make sure that the dependence of contractors on a single-platform employer is traced and triggers the

---

[5] The distinction between redistribution after, before, and in the market is developed in IPSP (2018a, Chapter 3).

activation of appropriate stakeholder rights. Fortunately, the technology that makes the platforms possible can also make it possible for contractors to coordinate and make their interests more visible and more seriously taken into account by the platforms themselves. But this will again require public authorities to see to it that such coordination occurs.

In such debates about the future of labor, the idea of a universal basic income occupies a central place.[6] There is a lot of exaggeration about this idea, because there are many forms in which a universal guarantee of income can be provided, and whether this guarantee is unconditional or means-tested is not negligible but not really world-changing. Indeed, people's income must be assessed anyway when they pay their taxes. So, the difference between a means-tested minimum income and an unconditional basic income is about whether the adjustment of government transfers as a function of an individual's pre-tax income takes place when determining the income support granted to this individual or when determining the income taxes paid (or tax credits received) by this individual. However, this makes a real difference in practice for the poor households whose earnings fluctuate. The delays of adjustment of income support are a nightmare for them, and the justification of their lack of income to social workers can be painful and humiliating. For this reason, a universal basic income is much better for the neediest households than a means-tested form of income support. This is a strong justification for unconditional forms of support.

The designers of welfare state systems in the last century did not have to deal with the environmental problem with the same urgency as nowadays. In order to deal with the sustainability problem, any model of welfare state should now incorporate a thorough management of externalities. Environmental but also social externalities are pervasive, and generate inefficient allocations of resources. If taxes

---

[6] Van Parijs and Vanderborght (2017) provide a comprehensive synthesis of the debate about the basic income.

and subsidies helped private decision-makers internalize the external effects of their choices, the economy could be much more efficient. This opens the prospect of reducing distortionary taxation, because taxes on externalities could generate revenue and enhance the efficiency of the economy at the same time. A carbon tax alone, in the range recommended by experts in climate policy, would generate more than 2 percent of GDP for several decades during the decarbonization process. Fossil fuels are still subsidized in many developing countries, with regressive impact because the rich benefit more from them, so that phasing them out and using the proceeds for poverty-relief policies would be good both for the environment and for the distribution of resources.[7]

Another source of revenue that would be efficiency-enhancing rather than distortionary is taxing rents, i.e. incomes that do not reward productive contribution but only the holding of scarce resources or advantageous positions. Urban land rents, which increase with economic development, can be captured by adequate taxation, encouraging a more efficient use of space, and can be used in particular to fund infrastructures. Monopolistic profits which are not justified by the need to reward innovation by patents, and cannot be fully eliminated by anti-trust policy, could be taxed as well through a modulation of corporate taxes, and this would discourage excessive concentration. Similarly, rent-seeking activities which are not really creating value but aim at capturing value, such as advertising,[8] lobbying, and a proportion of financial[9] and litigation businesses,

---

[7] On carbon policy and social impacts, see Stern and Stiglitz (2017) and Edenhofer et al. (2017), and references therein.

[8] Advertising is a prominent example in Pigou's seminal book *The Economics of Welfare* (1920), which introduced the idea of taxing externalities. Indeed, observe that advertising is not only a rent-seeking activity, but it is also a nuisance for businesses which are drawn into a wasteful arms race against each other to attract customers.

[9] The famous Tobin tax in particular would target short-term speculation by taxing financial transactions, encouraging investors to hold on to their investments for a longer time.

among others, could be submitted to taxation designed to contain their expansion (see Chapter 6).

All this will not be sufficient to replace taxes on labor, but it can substantially reduce the deadweight of such distortionary taxes. This would contribute to orienting technological innovation in a more socially beneficial direction, because the prices (including taxes) would better reflect the social impacts of decisions about processes and products.

Can the new welfare state model face the globalized economy? Like social democracy, it is compatible with borders open to trade and capital investment. Of course, the political outlook of democratic principles imposed on businesses may initially frighten investors and managers. However, the only real constraint as far as capital flight is concerned is guaranteeing the same level of profitability as elsewhere, and this constraint can be treated in the same way as a tax by any productive firm requesting capital investment or any bank borrowing on international markets. Highly skilled workers, such as managers, can be tempted by higher wages abroad but there are real advantages to a friendly work environment and a socially cohesive society, and this will convince many to stay – in fact, even top managers usually stay in their country. Observe, for instance, that democratic politics does not make the job of politician less attractive in democracies than in authoritarian governments, and it certainly makes it safer. Similarly, in the current capitalist economy in which democratic firms have to compete with traditional authoritarian firms, they are not particularly short of volunteers for management positions – and they need less intermediate management. Interestingly, the parallel between politics and business extends also to the fact that in both contexts, democratic structures promote a different type of manager – less predatory, more humane, though potentially demagogic.

In conclusion, the welfare state not only remains a viable idea in the twenty-first century, but it can be a key player in promoting social progress, focused not just on securing people's livelihoods, but also on guaranteeing their dignity, freedom, and democratic rights, while contributing to an efficient market economy.

8   From Polaritics to Politics

In the previous two chapters, we have seen how reforming the corporation and the markets and developing an emancipating state could shape the contours of a better society. Does the political system also need reforms?

The situation in politics has become more and more worrisome lately, due to growing polarization in many democratic countries, which does not bode well for the future of democracy, and has transformed the noble confrontation of platforms into a nasty wrestling show that could be dubbed "polaritics." Polarization is associated with social trends that drive populations apart. In some countries, the clash opposes well-endowed (economically and culturally) elites to populations left behind who fall prey to identity politics. In other countries, the clash is a more classical left–right, worker–elite, opposition, but in all countries, identity politics and the consequences of globalization (and secondarily technological change) are part of the equation. In particular, many citizens now think that their government is a puppet in the hands of global economic and financial forces and that changing the government does not bring any substantial change in policies. Endorsement of democracy remains strong but seems to be eroding, especially among young generations (see Figure 8.1). Relatedly, in many countries, corruption issues pollute the political game so much that they become a central concern for imagining healthier democratic systems.

The socio-economic reforms proposed in the previous chapters are themselves political, since they actually involve inoculating germs of good politics in economic activities where power is at stake, as well as in social policies where the recipients are key stakeholders. They involve acknowledging the presence of politics in domains

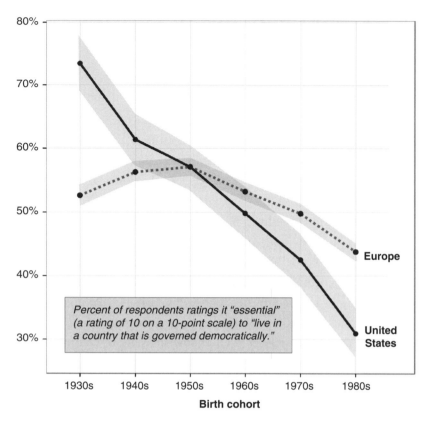

FIGURE 8.1 Eroding Support for Democratic Institutions in Younger
Generations
Source: Foa and Mounk (2016, fig. 1).

which are not in the classical political sphere, and deepening democratization as an essential driver of social progress in the economy, in
civil society, in families, and in social policy. Politics is everywhere
because power is ubiquitous.

Still, a good society needs a good political sphere, and conversely, politics thrives when social conditions are favorable. In
this chapter we first explain why and how social progress and political progress are intertwined, and then discuss ideas for improving
the political system. Reforms are needed in the funding of political

activities, the participation of citizens in decision-making, the organization and management of the media, and the electoral process.

Defining how to improve politics is not the end of our story, however. We still need to identify the actions and the actors who can push and contribute to making possible all the changes described in this second part of the book. This will be the topic of the last chapter, after this one.

SOCIAL PROGRESS AND POLITICAL PROGRESS

It takes two to tango. Social progress needs political support, and political progress needs a favorable social environment.

Why does social progress need politics? This may seem obvious for the conventional view that conflates social progress and income redistribution by the government, but for the sort of socially diffuse progress proposed in this book, this is not so obvious. Consider for instance the reform of the purpose and governance of the corporation discussed in Chapter 6. Such a reform can be pushed by social movements and by the initiative of the most enlightened part of the business community, so why invoke state support? The reason is that, at some point, the generalization of the reform and its crystallization in robust institutions requires legal backing, otherwise deviations away from democracy will remain pervasive. It may seem suspect that more democratic organizations need legal safeguards to survive in a competitive world. Could this prove that they are actually less efficient than traditional corporations that maximize shareholder value with a strong management?

As a matter of fact, there is every reason to think that competition does not necessarily select the best form of organization. It does typically select the best organizations in the eyes of those who hold the levers of the selection mechanism, for sure, but their interests may not correspond to the common good. In the case of firms, it may seem that the selection is mainly done by consumers, i.e., by everyone. The best firms are, then, those that are the most productive and are able to propose the lowest prices. Or one could think that the workers also contribute to selecting the firms, moving to those with better wages and working conditions, whereas the less efficient firms will struggle to attract good workers.

But this is not quite the case. Neither the consumers nor the workers really play a big role. The birth, life, and death of firms are primarily determined by their ability to attract funding and to generate profits. Now, profits are only a small part of the value created by the collective contributions of capital, sweat, and wit made by the stakeholders. If there are two types of firms, with one generating a greater value but with smaller profits than the other, it is the latter type, unfortunately, that will be selected. The fact that more democratic firms will create more value but smaller profits is indeed likely, due to the fact that the size of the pie is not independent of how it is distributed. A more democratic firm designs its system of rewards in a way that reduces the gap between the executives and the ordinary workers; it provides better working conditions which foster labor productivity but also include perks to workers in the form of job stability, accommodations of family life, and the like; and it adopts a more cautious policy when profitable opportunities clash with environmental concerns. All of this, on average, reduces monetary profits for shareholders while enhancing the total value created.

Imagine that by the strike of a magic wand, all firms became democratic, but without legal safeguards protecting the stakeholders' rights. What would happen? Most firms would degenerate back into the classical form. Democracy without safeguards is not viable, and this is true in every context. The problem with democracy is that it is a public good, and like any public good, one cannot rely on its emergence and survival being spontaneous. When the organization you are a member of is democratic, you benefit from your interests being taken into account and if you don't participate, others like you will do it for you. And when the organization is not democratic, there is little you can do by yourself to change it. So, whatever the context, it is never in your personal interest to spend much effort to create or protect democracy, unless you are a strong, committed idealist.

In the political sphere, likewise, democracy does not survive when votes can be bought freely by the wealthy. For the poor voters, what is the point of retaining an individual voting right which changes nothing about the election results, when some real money can be earned by selling it? In the labor market, workers who sign a labor contract similarly sell their dignity as stakeholders when they accept the subordination stipulated in the contract. And they sell it for nothing, given that the pressure of unemployment makes them accept working for almost any kind of organization.

In summary, and generalizing beyond the example of firms, social progress that takes the form of democratization everywhere needs political and legal support, and therefore a favorable political system.

Conversely, politics works well only when the social context is healthy. Historical experience repeatedly shows that populations who suffer from social and economic distress are more vulnerable to extremist sirens proposing quick and radical, but treacherous, fixes to their predicament. Moreover, when inequality grows it becomes easier and more profitable for the elite to capture the political system (IPSP 2018b, chapters 9 and 14). It becomes easier because with greater resources it is possible to lobby or corrupt politicians, to support their campaigns and parties in such a weighty way that they feel obligated to reciprocate, or to get access to the public sphere via the media. Moreover, politicians themselves often come from the elite and therefore tend to naturally adopt the views of the super-rich when the elite counts more super-rich among its ranks. It also becomes more profitable because the stakes are higher when the interests to defend are stratospheric and when the redistribution system is lax and leaves more of the gains to fall into the hands of the racketeers. Vicious circles can then unfold, in which the interests of the most privileged become entrenched in a distorted political process that protects them and repeatedly advances their interests (Bartels 2016).

GETTING MONEY OUT OF POLITICS?

To break such vicious circles, getting money out of politics seems a key component of any effective strategy. This is, for some political activities, mission impossible. Billionaires like Charles Koch and George Soros fund think tanks and civil society movements, and little can be done to avoid such political "philanthropy." But imposing norms of transparency in the funding of all political activities, including think tanks and grassroots movements, could go a long way toward clarifying the situation and curbing the worst abuses – as already mentioned in Chapter 6.

For instance, when big tobacco in the US reached a litigation settlement in 1998 with forty-six states, the settlement included various restrictions on tobacco advertising and financial compensations for medical expenses, but, most interestingly, it also forced the tobacco majors to release tons of internal documents. These documents recently revealed how a long-term alliance between the Koch brothers and tobacco money, initiated in the Reagan years under the Coalition for Fiscal Restraint, has been operating in secrecy, especially since Bill Clinton's election, to fabricate a popular movement against taxes and against government. Many campaigns, groups, and think tanks, such as Citizens Against Regressive Taxation, Enough Is Enough, Get Government Off Our Back, Citizens for a Sound Economy (rebranded Americans for Prosperity in 2006), or the Sam Adams Alliance, got millions of dollars from a completely opaque network orchestrated by big oil (the Kochs in particular) and big tobacco, over many years, and ultimately succeeded in creating a grassroots movement, the Tea Party, which appeared to emerge from nowhere in 2009, just after Obama's election.[1] Due to entrenched majorities in many electoral districts tailor-made for the Republicans by the Republicans in outrageous gerrymandering, the Tea Party has been able to carry primaries in

---

[1] The story of this long-term campaign is told in Nesbit (2016).

many states, creating a strong ultraconservative group in Congress. The current vice president, Mike Pence, is one of the few politicians intimate to the inner Koch circle. In many ways, the Tea Party is now in charge, both in the White House and on Capitol Hill. One can only speculate about how much difference it would have made if transparency about the funding of these pseudo-popular movements had been imposed, but it is likely that their political momentum and legitimacy would have been seriously undermined. Many people in the movements themselves would have realized that their anger against the government was being manipulated to serve big business interests rather than their own.

Other channels of money influence can be tackled more directly, perhaps, such as campaign funding and lobbying. Campaign funding is regulated in many different ways in various countries. Countries where important funding is provided by the state are mostly concentrated in Scandinavia, and this appears to reduce the dependency of politicians on big donors. In Russia, however, public money is used to favor the dominant party, allowing incumbents to campaign in official events and through biased media reporting. In Brazil and the US, as well as African countries like Nigeria, political parties overwhelmingly get their funding from corporations. The US has strict limits on direct donations to campaigns, but no limits on the funding of political action committees (PACs) producing TV ads and media campaigns favoring or fighting particular candidates. In the 2016 election cycle, more than 2,000 groups organized as "super PACs" reported total expenditures of more than a billion dollars. This must be added to the election cycle spending itself, around 1.5 billion dollars. In Brazil, private donations from individuals are negligible and most of the funding comes from corporations, which creates a vicious circle of distrust between citizens and politicians. The fight for transparency and against corruption seems endless in many countries.

The question of political influence through the media is the topic of a later section of this chapter. Regarding political funding itself, the difficulty of funding political activities generates an obvious temptation for corruption, since politicians are desperate for money and wealthy donors are keen to gain influence. How can politics be shielded from such temptations? One way of thinking about solutions is to view politics itself as a public good, as already explained in the previous section. Corruption is really damaging since it privatizes this public good by creating a market for political favors, undermining the search for the common good. Relying on small private donations to push the donors' favorite party or candidate still smacks of privatization of the political process. If a sound political system is a public good, it needs a coordinated system of funding with mandatory contributions.

Assuming such a system of central funding is in place, how to allocate the money, then? The Russian system of distribution of money and airtime in proportion to former results in the election suits a dominant party that crushes the opposition, and most systems of public funding include some form of "grand-fathering." An alternative option is to let citizens indicate how they would like the political budget to be spent, every year, and compute the average of their wishes. While the committed partisans would advocate spending the whole budget on their own party, if they behave strategically, the independent voters may add some nuance and propose balanced shares. Overall, the final budget would reflect the numbers (not the wealth) of partisans and the more balanced preferences of the independent.

Let us now turn to lobbying. Lobbying is a multi-billion-dollar industry by itself in certain decision centers such as Washington DC or Brussels, and one of its most shocking features is the revolving door between civil service and lobbying firms, transforming civil servants supposedly dedicated to the common good into special interest agents selling their insider knowledge, and back. The frontier between lobbying and corruption is very thin, since personal relations developed between politicians and lobbyists generate connivance that, even without explicit bribes, destroys the objectivity of the legislative work. The situation is complex because many domains in which politicians elaborate laws and regulations are quite technical and require the expertise of the industry itself. It is therefore hard to disentangle the necessary exchange of information from problematic pressure on politicians to sympathize with the industry's interests. In the same vein, lobbying also operates surreptitiously through expert studies made by think tanks with opaque corporate funding. Tobacco and alcohol producers have spent millions of dollars to fund studies that pretended to debunk epidemiological results showing the dangers of these drugs. The concentration of industries into oligopolies of giant firms has made things worse, since such firms have much more money and ability to coordinate lobbying actions.

The typical measures taken to regulate lobbying include registering lobbyists. In the US, registering and declaration of amounts spent is mandatory, unlike in Brussels, where it is voluntary. As a consequence, official numbers suggest that lobbying in the EU is dwarfed by the US lobbying industry, but this is probably just because of under-declaration in the EU industry. Another important measure involves mandatory delays and cooling periods in the revolving door system. Needless to say, corporations resist such measures as much as possible, and even civil servants show little enthusiasm for cooling periods that reduce their prospects of well-paid jobs in the private sector.

The problem with lobbying is that even if it were transparent and "clean," it would generate a bias in the process of political deliberations. "It provides corporations with a mechanism to have their demands and their world view attended to while the demands of the public have no such forum" (IPSP 2018a, chapter 6). Therefore, decisive action against the harmful effects of lobbying should not be limited to lobbying itself but also target how policy is made, in the political deliberative and decision process. Checking the channels of information and influence in the political offices and setting up specific forums for ordinary citizens and especially for the least advantaged social groups are of paramount importance. The latter is the topic of the next section.

REPRESENTATION, PARTICIPATION, DELIBERATION

The debate about the pros and cons of representative versus direct democracy has been going on forever, i.e. at least since the Ancient Greeks. Representative democracy runs the risk of representatives becoming a new class with specific interests, somewhat disconnected from the average citizen. But representatives can also build specific skills in handling public affairs, and there are many examples of amateurism turning sour when "real" people get brought to the political turf. Recent mishaps with the Five Star Movement in Italy have illustrated the difficulty of improvising in politics, and the similar experiment to renew political personnel attempted by the recently elected president of France should be watched carefully too.

Direct democracy, in contrast, bets on the wisdom of the crowd, and the possibility for referenda and similar votes to directly make decisions on key policy issues. There is obviously a presumption in favor of direct votes on issues to better represent the opinion of the polity at the time of the vote. Whether this opinion is stable and reasonable is, of course, another matter. Populists generally like to promote referenda because they hope to use them as plebiscites and expect the electorate to endorse their simplistic solutions involving harsh treatment of scapegoats such as wealthy or poor citizens, criminals, minorities, and immigrants. Yet, it seems patronizing to believe that the crowd is generally stupid and easily manipulated, if the alternative is to have a clique of political professionals capture the state and run it to its own benefit. As illustrated in Table 8.1, in the USA, the preferences of the wealthy, which have a strong impact on those of politicians, appear to differ substantially from those of the average citizen, so that a representative democracy in which most representatives are themselves wealthy or under the influence of the wealthy may not be the best way to fulfill the polity's desires.

Table 8.1 *Policy Preferences of the Wealthy and the General Public, USA*

Issues	Wealthy support	General public support
The federal government should spend whatever is necessary to ensure that all children have really good public schools they can go to	35 percent	87 percent
The federal government should make sure that everyone who wants to go to college can do so	28 percent	78 percent
Minimum wage high enough so that no family with a full-time worker falls below the official poverty line	40 percent	78 percent
The government in Washington ought to see to it that everyone who wants to work can find a job	19 percent	68 percent
Government must see that no one is without food, clothing, or shelter	43 percent	68 percent
Favor national health insurance, which would be financed by tax money, paying for most forms of health care	32 percent	61 percent
Favor cuts in spending on domestic programs like Medicare, education, and highways in order to cut federal budget deficits	58 percent	27 percent

Source: Bartels (2016); 2011 Survey of Economically Successful Americans (for wealthy Americans); contemporaneous public surveys (for general public).

Fortunately, it is possible to go beyond the simplistic opposition between representative and direct democracy. Deliberative-participative democracy is a form of democracy in which representatives and citizens interact not just during elections but also in decision procedures in which citizens are involved in conditions that are similar to parliamentary work. They receive expertise, have the time to discuss and deliberate, and make recommendations based on this work instead of just casting a ballot reflecting their gut feelings. This deliberative work cannot be done by the whole citizenry at the same time, and has to rely on small panels of citizens who can be drawn by lot or volunteer, or even be elected for a short and specific mandate. There is a continuum of formulae that range from parliamentary democracy with severe term limits on representatives to multiple citizen juries dedicated to specific issues.

A famous example is participatory budgeting, initiated by Porto Alegre in Brazil in 1989 and now practiced all over the world in thousands of cities. It involves different assemblies and elected committees making demands and allocating dedicated funds according to rules endorsed by the citizens.

> The attractiveness of participatory budgeting, particularly in Latin America, is tied particularly to its capacity to generate a more equitable redistribution of public goods and to increase the levels of participation among disadvantaged groups, the less educated and lower-income citizens. There is evidence that participatory budgeting improves social wellbeing, with increased spending in health care and decreases in infant mortality rates across Brazil's 253 largest cities. (IPSP 2018b, chapter 14)

Latin America has been very much at the forefront of democratic innovation, with many other forms of participation such as deliberative councils created to address particular issues, management councils dedicated to specific domains such as health care, representative councils giving voice to underrepresented minorities, and national public policy conferences which are multilevel deliberation structures for citizens and civil society organizations. Western countries have experimented with mini-publics in many areas (including constitutional issues in Canada, the Netherlands, Iceland, and Ireland). Stratified selection is often used in mini-publics to ensure the presence of politically excluded social groups.

Promising as these democratic innovations are, the challenge is to codify them to ensure their integrity (participatory budgeting in Europe is often a pale imitation of the initial Latin-American model) while preserving the possibility of innovation. One interesting formula is the creation of autonomous public organizations dedicated to public participation. They are created by governments with the mandate to organize or oversee democratic innovations in specified areas of policy. Examples include the Danish Teknologiraadet, the French Commission nationale du débat public, the Montreal Office de consultation publique, and the Tuscany Autorità regionale per la garanzia e la promozione della partecipazione. Their "degree of autonomy and visibility … protects them to some extent from day-to-day political pressures, ensuring a degree of quality and oversight of participatory arrangements and a competent authority to promote the outcomes of democratic innovations within decision-making processes" (IPSP 2018b, chapter 14).

THE FOURTH POWER

The media play a crucial role in politics, and beyond. They provide the foundation for a collective understanding of group identities and of ongoing events, and their responsibility in framing people's perceptions of social issues cannot be overstated. For instance, deaths from terrorism get much more press coverage than female deaths from partner assault, even if the numbers of the latter (about 10 percent of total homicides, more or less evenly spread in the world) dwarf the former (about 5 percent worldwide, most of which in the Middle East and Asia; see IPSP 2018b, chapter 10). For instance, a woman born in the USA has roughly 500 more chances of being killed by her partner than by a terrorist, but the media rarely mention this.[2] In the countries in which religious authorities do not intervene much in public debates, the media inherit an ideological authority that can either respect the plurality of views in society or promote a more unified vision serving whoever controls their editorial line. The media have a long history of being contested, when they appeared biased and subservient to state or wealthy interests, but also of being channels of contestation of the authorities, serving the cause of democracy. Amartya Sen (1981), in his analysis of famines, considers a free press one of the most important factors of prevention, due to their role in exposing bad management and social deprivation.

The traditional press is now struggling under the pressure of the new media, in particular social networks such as Facebook, Twitter, and independent blogs. The new media reinforce the phenomenon of ideological tribes. It was, of course, always possible to select a newspaper or a radio channel of one's liking, but the number of options was more limited. More importantly, nowadays, the number of producers of news is multiplied and includes all sorts of people, whose intentions may be less pure than the typical journalist's. Rumors, conspiracy theories, and fake news are now propagated much more quickly and in staggering proportions, compelling the serious media to divert part of their resources to debunking them, even if they can hardly reach the most gullible customers of such rumors. At the same time, the new media amplify the possibilities of coordination of social movements and have played an important role in the Arab Spring, as well as in exposing police abuse and other scandals that can be captured on video.

Another consequence of the restructuring of the media is a movement of concentration in many countries, producing large conglomerates of media and communications. Media businesspeople and politicians become increasingly close, and some influential politicians have a background as important media owners, such as

---

[2] There are exceptions, of course. See, e.g., www.businessinsider.fr/us/death-risk-statistics-terrorism-disease-accidents-2017-1/ or http://edition.cnn.com/2016/10/03/us/terrorism-gun-violence/.

Hary Tanoesoedibjo in Indonesia and Silvio Berlusconi in Italy, or media producers, such as Donald Trump in the USA. In addition, a new digital industry of data collection tracks the online behavior of the population and sells it for profit to businesses which can use it to target advertising and similar commercial operations. Citizens are increasingly wary of being under close cyber-surveillance, either by the state or by businesses.[3]

A related negative trend is the pervasiveness of the media in the political game itself. Every government, political party, and ambitious politician increasingly employs the services of professional media gurus, marketing people, and spin doctors. Ezrahi (1990) has called this a shift from "state-craft" to "stage-craft." Politics has become a public stage, directed by attention-grabbing headlines and Twitter messages – a mixture of staged entertainment and emitting carefully crafted messages that Machiavelli would have been proud of.

This complex evolving pattern of concentration and corporatization of the traditional media and diffuse growth of the production of low-cost, low-quality news raises a serious challenge for democracy. How to protect the citizen against the influence of big business controlling big media, as well as against the fakers who propagate a stew of distorted news, sometimes under the impulsion of rogue states? At the same time, one would like to retain the amplification of citizens' voice made possible by greater access to news producing and sharing.

To tackle these trends, inspiration can come once again from Latin America. After the Snowden scandal, Brazil developed a regulatory initiative called the Marco Civil da Internet (Civil Rights Framework for the Internet), through a large participatory process involving civil society organizations and citizens. It "considers

---

[3] For instance, "in 2015, the Indian government launched the Digital India Initiative, which is based on the use of the Aadhar Unique Identity scheme for biometric authentication of recipients of government benefits and services. The Aadhar scheme, which is the world's largest biometrics-based database initiative, was developed by corporate technology partners, and critics charge that too little is known about its capabilities and potential future uses" (IPSP 2018b, chapter 13).

access to the internet fundamental to democracy, as it is essential for participation in political life and cultural production, and part of the right to education and freedom of expression," and it includes "the protection of freedom and privacy, open governance, universal inclusion, cultural diversity, and network neutrality" (IPSP 2018, chapter 13).

The guiding principle for reform in this domain, then, is that, given its role in educating and informing citizens and providing the core arena for public debate, the media and communication infrastructure should be considered a common good, which is hardly compatible with the standard media business model driven by consumer demand and advertising revenues. This means that its governance and regulation should be open and participatory, that the independence and neutrality of the key institutions and actors should be preserved both from state overbearing and business embezzlement, and that access to content production should be guaranteed to all, especially minorities and disadvantaged groups. There is no simple institutional formula implementing all of this in an automatic way, and a combination of public and crowd-funding of non-profit media, certification mechanisms, and independent and participatory monitoring bodies has to be imagined and adapted to every local situation.[4]

WHAT ABOUT REFORMING THE ELECTORAL SYSTEM?

Politics in many countries also suffers from electoral rules that fail the electorate, betraying the population's wishes and putting into office governments that do not reflect the popular views.

The USA provides an interesting example, with an apparent bias in favor of Republicans (Table 8.2). Twice in the short history of the twenty-first century, a Republican president was elected with a minority of the popular vote. The ill-famed electoral college is responsible for this mismatch. The irony is that this college was created to protect the government from the popular temptation to

---

[4] A more detailed action plan is proposed in IPSP (2018b, chapter 13).

Table 8.2 *Votes and Election Results in the USA*

Date	President					Senate				House		
	Dem	Rep	Elected			Dem	Rep	Majority		Dem	Rep	Majority
2016	**48.2%**	**46.1%**	**Rep**			**53.8%**	**42.4%**	**Rep**		45.5%	51.2%	Rep
2012	51.1%	47.2%	Dem			53.7%	42.1%	Dem		**48.3%**	**46.9%**	**Rep**
2008	52.9%	45.6%	Dem			50.8%	44.2%	Dem		52.9%	42.3%	Dem
2004	48.3%	50.7%	Rep			**50.6%**	**46.3%**	**Rep**		46.5%	49.0%	Rep
2000	**48.4%**	**47.9%**	**Rep**			46.4%	46.3%	Dem		46.8%	47.0%	Rep

Source: Federal Electoral Commission for 2000–2012; Wikipedia for 2016.

vote for demagogues, and actually permitted the election of Trump against popular votes. And the Congress is controlled by Republicans more often than it should be in view of popular votes. Moreover, Republicans have gerrymandered congressional districts to obtain large majorities in the House and even be shielded from reversals of popular vote, as observed for instance in 2012.[5]

The emergence of Trump in the Republican primaries is attributed to the plurality system that favors the candidate with the strongest backing in the polls, even if he or she is disliked by a majority of voters. Similarly, in France, plurality selects the two top candidates in the first round of the presidential election. As a consequence, the extreme right-wing National Front is able to disturb presidential elections by reaching the second round of a run-off election, even though there is a robust majority of voters who strongly dislike this party. This has already happened twice, in 2002 and 2017. The impact of the National Front on the public debate is then magnified by its potential role in this silly electoral formula. This amplifies xenophobic and anti-European discourse in other parties. In the UK, plurality with only one round ("first past the post") has also entrenched a two-party system that severely constrains the expression of political opinions. It is possible for a party that barely dominates the others and obtains not much more than a third of the votes to govern the country with a strong majority of seats in Westminster, as has happened since 2005.

A two-round election formula is used in forty countries around the world, and the first-past-the-post system is used in fifty-eight countries. Is it possible to avoid the instability of plurality that undermines the legitimacy of such electoral rules? Recent research

---

[5] For a balanced analysis of the role of gerrymandering in the late political era, see J.E. Zelizer, "The Power that Gerrymandering Has Brought to Republicans," Washington Post, June 17, 2016. www.washingtonpost.com/opinions/the-power-that-gerrymandering-has-brought-to-republicans/2016/06/17/045264ae-2903-11e6-ae4a-3cdd5fe74204_story.html?utm_term=.a48864ea72aa.

has provided a resounding yes in answer to this question. Beyond introducing more proportionate parliamentary representation based on the actual distribution of votes across political parties, there are voting rules that enable voters to approve several candidates or to grade them. Such rules appear much better at capturing political preferences. The simplest of such rules asks the voter to grade candidates with only two grades: approved and not approved. The winner of the election is the candidate getting the most approvals (Brams and Fishburn 1983). A more sophisticated rule offers a richer list of grades, such as excellent, good, acceptable, fair, mediocre, and bad, and attributes to every candidate the highest grade such that a majority of the electorate gave the candidate this or a better grade. The selected candidate is the one with the greatest percentage of support among those with the highest grade (Balinski and Laraki 2011 propose a variant of this rule). For instance, if Candidate X gets the grade "acceptable" or better from 52 percent of the voters, whereas Candidate Y gets the grade "acceptable" or better from 53 percent, and no candidate gets a better grade from more than 50 percent, then Candidate Y is elected. What is interesting about this rule is that voters have limited incentives to misrepresent their opinions, since this will generally not change the result (Candidate Y does not get greater chance of being elected if a supporter gives her an "excellent" rather than "good" or "acceptable"). Also, the elected candidate not only gets the job but also an approval rating in the form of a grade, indicating how he or she stands in the voters' esteem.

These rules have been experimented with, and results show that they reduce the role of minority candidates such as the National Front in France, and they tend to favor centrist candidates, thereby offering a way to reduce the polarization of politics.

Another thorny issue is abstention and registration of voters. In the USA, this is a very strategic issue. The suppression of the black vote has been cynically pursued by making registering and voting hard for working people in poor districts (voting always occurs during a working day, ID requirements penalize people without a passport or driver's license, and long lines are more frequent in poor districts), as well as by mass incarceration of blacks accompanied by the exclusion of felons and former felons from registers. In many countries, the voices of the poor are less influential because they participate less in the elections. There is a simple solution to this problem: make voting compulsory, and make it easy. Currently only 22 percent of countries have compulsory voting rules, and only half of them enforce these rules. There are no convincing arguments against compulsory voting, since it is always possible to cast a blank vote if one is not satisfied with the options.

Other changes in the electoral rules that may have a significant impact involve strict term limits to curb the numbers of the caste of professional politicians. This has already been mentioned in a previous section.

In conclusion, even if the best service to political democracy that we could do is to give it a sound social environment in the form of the just society, there are many specific reforms that could be implemented to improve national politics: fighting corruption and lobbying, reforming campaign finance, enhancing citizen participation in decision-making, democratizing media and communications viewed as a common good, and adopting better electoral systems.

Beyond rejuvenating national and local politics, should we also aim at building a global democracy? Large federal systems, as in Brazil and the USA, or international unions like Europe, struggle with the fact that many citizens feel estranged from the center. Yet, many decisions require global cooperation and coordination, so that a permanent body of decision-makers representing the world citizens would be arguably better than the shallow consultation arenas provided by the United Nations. One could hope that direct participation of citizens in central elections would offer a better outlook than multilayer systems in which voters have no direct influence on the selection of the decision-makers in the center. However, the

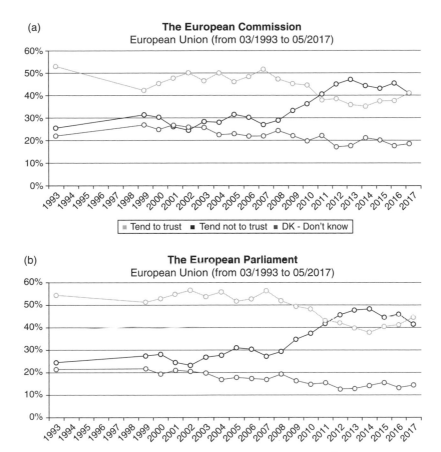

FIGURE 8.2 Declining Trust in European Institutions
Source: Eurobarometer. http://ec.europa.eu/commfrontoffice/
publicopinion/index.cfm/Chart/index.

European parliament, for instance, does not look like a success story, since the turnout in elections has stayed below 50 percent since 1999, and its approval rating is not much better than that of the non-elected European Commission or the indirectly representative Council of Ministers (see Figure 8.2). Large-scale democracy remains a challenging area where new institutions must be imagined.

Conclusion: Mobilizing Change-Makers

This book has celebrated the great achievements of past centuries of development, warned against the looming dangers that threaten the foundations of our societies and ecosystems, and offered a positive vision of a possible future, in which the market economy would be re-embedded in social institutions pursuing social justice and sustainability. If we can bridge the chasm opened by looming catastrophes and transition to a new set of institutions that jointly promote equity, sustainability, and democracy, we can hope for a continuation of social progress in the foreseeable future.

But bridging the chasm will not happen simply if a few or even most people see the bright vision on the other side. A desirable future may be realistic and viable, but it may remain a utopia if the obstacles to the transition are too big. And the obstacles are indeed formidable. They take the form of powerful vested interests promoting a persistently strong TINA discourse, a dominant culture generally favoring short-termism, mesmerized mobs following demagogues, failures to cooperate due to obtuse selfishness, education systems replicating yesterday's assumptions and mental structures, and sheer stupidity and bigotry.

So, we need not just a vision but also a strategy. The authors of this book are not political strategists, but this is not about launching a new party. The stakes are larger, deeper. And the message we want to convey in this chapter is that *everyone* can contribute to the desired transformation. We believe that the transformation that is needed will only happen through a grassroots push. This concluding chapter explains why and how.

WHO RULES THE WORLD?

Who Rules the World? is the title of one of Noam Chomsky's books, in which he criticizes the nefarious role of the United States, and especially the CIA, in international geopolitics. The broader question of who really holds power in world affairs, not just in geopolitics but in economic and social affairs as well, is one that has rattled many thinkers and remains largely open. Conspiracy adepts from the left have had their eyes not just on the CIA but also on the World Economic Forum, the Trilateral Commission, and similar think tanks, while conspiracy adepts from the right look at financial centers in the dark tradition of anti-Semitic fantasies. In *Who Governs?*, the political scientist Robert Dahl asked a similar question about the city of New Haven in Connecticut: "In a political system where nearly every adult may vote but where knowledge, wealth, social position, access to officials, and other resources are unequally distributed, who actually governs?" (1961, p. 1). Perhaps surprisingly, he found out that power was actually spread over many groups and was not in the hands of a small oligarchy. He coined the word "polyarchy" to describe the situation in which power is not concentrated within any single well-knit group.

It is most likely that the distribution of power in the world, nowadays, is a polyarchy, even if business interests have the upper hand on many issues or at least, as in New Haven in the 1950s, can block developments that they perceive as potentially harming their profits. But the important point we want to make here is that, even if power was concentrated, what would matter anyway is a different question: Who can change society? Those who hold power may not actually be able to change society. Most probably, they can only – and most of them only want to – preserve a certain status quo. And conversely, those who can change society need not belong to the hypothetical oligarchy that might have power over current affairs.

How can this paradox come about? It is partly a matter of timing. Those who hold power over current affairs have a short- to medium-term horizon and cannot control the deeper changes in structures, cultures, and behaviors that slowly go on in the layers of society. In the long run, society follows movements that are largely initiated by large groups of people with similar interests and who push for change, bit by bit, until the dam breaks or the ground slides.

Take for instance the spectacular change of women's condition in many countries over the last century. One century ago, most women had no voting right, were considered legal minors on a par with children in their households, and were almost completely dependent on males for their survival and reproductive life, unless they joined a female religious order where freedom was also very limited. Even if their situation remains very imperfect today, and even if some countries have stayed behind, the transformation has been absolutely life-changing for many women. Lately, even the daily disrespect and harassment that women have endured is under serious pressure. Could such a sea change have been initiated by the hypothetical oligarchy, certainly composed of old males at least when the change started? This seems most unlikely. It was the relentless pressure of women themselves that changed norms. True, they were helped by technological innovation (contraception) and historical accidents (war efforts requiring female labor force), but they were at the front line of historic battles for voting rights, reproductive rights, and access to professions. The recent #MeToo wave has been carried by women's initiative all along.

The lesson of these remarks is therefore clear: even if you don't belong to the (real or imaginary) oligarchy, you can make a contribution toward improving society, not only around you, but indirectly on a large scale.

TWO ADDITIONAL REASONS TO GO GRASSROOTS

Many deep changes in society involve the long-run evolution of behaviors and norms. For instance, the adoption of particular languages for international communication is rarely a top-down decision but slowly emerges through multiple decisions and occasions where various practices are tested. Once a language emerges as the most common *lingua franca*, it becomes attractive for more people to learn it, reinforcing the pre-eminence of this particular language.

But the change we are interested in here is especially prone to require the involvement of the stakeholders. Indeed, the vision of social progress we propose in this book is largely a matter of empowering individuals and groups, expanding the scope of democracy and deepening its mechanisms. This cannot be fully realized without the participation of the stakeholders themselves. Moreover, it is unlikely to be even initiated without a push from them. There may exist examples of generous autocrats who, out of benevolence, decide to share their power. But we will not venture to provide many examples here, because there is always the suspicion that such moves are also meant to preempt a looming crisis in which their position would have been openly contested. Perhaps the business world is where such plausible examples can be found, because the authoritarian culture is so dominant in that world that the entrepreneurs who decide to democratize their management are unlikely to have been submitted to serious pressure to do so. Dane Atkinson, the founder of a big data company writes:

> When my co-founders and I launched SumAll four years
> ago we decided we didn't want to work in an evil, miserable
> environment. When people have crappy managers and deceitful
> executives, they start to hate life, and things get evil quickly.
> So, we came up with a solution: Let employees elect their own
> leaders and make all managers accountable to the people they
> manage; if leaders can't earn respect and loyalty, they shouldn't
> be leading a team.[1]

This kind of example is not rare, but more often, democratization comes from the boiling pressure of the crowd. In other words, there is

---

[1] https://techcrunch.com/2015/07/21/executives-and-managers-should-all-be-elected/.

a type of social progress that is especially likely to require a bottom-up process, and this is precisely the type of progress we propose here.

Another reason to believe in a bottom-up process is that there are so many possibilities for improving institutions that a central direction for social experimenting is unlikely to work. It is much more realistic to imagine a scenario in which many local initiatives test ideas coming from the field, and those that are successful can then serve as lead examples that inspire followers and secondary innovations. Cities, most notably the largest ones, can play a significant role, as we have seen with the C40 on climate change or in many countries on migration issues. In the previous chapters, this book has not proposed a single system, but only general ideas of directions that can be pursued in different domains. These ideas can be embodied in multiple forms, and there is a tremendous need to improve our knowledge of what works through social experiments. Many such experiments can be local – at the community or at the city levels – even if some do require more general coordination. Moreover, different contexts require different solutions, due to specific cultures and traditions, or to specific technological and economic possibilities. The diversity of solutions adapted to local contexts cannot be fathomed by a central leadership, and requires bottom-up initiative and control.[2]

We have therefore identified three reasons to encourage everyone to take initiative: (1) Deep societal changes come from people, social movements and civil society organizations, rarely from top leaders; (2) This is especially true for democratization and empowerment, which require the participation of, and generally a push by, the stakeholders; (3) Many experiments are needed to explore how to implement and adapt general ideas to local needs and possibilities.

---

[2] For instance, religious groups, due to their networks and dedication to social causes, can be valuable partners with other organizations and with public authorities in developing social actions (IPSP 2018c, chapter 16).

THINK GLOBAL

One key caveat is that one should not understand grassroots as meaning "small" and "local." On the contrary, it is now increasingly important to think big and global. The slogan "think global, act local" has been popular for a long time and encourages local initiatives for sustainability, especially in urban design. But it is now outdated. By coordinating initiatives, it is not just thought but also action that can become global and be amplified in its impact. "Think global" now should mean: think of global action whenever possible.

One of the main inequalities that nowadays generate considerable imbalance in power and opportunities is that the elite is global, at ease everywhere, while the left-behind are grounded in a local world, unable to understand people beyond a narrow circle. In fact, this vision opposing the "everywhere" people to the "here" people is simplistic. In reality, simple people know that the elite is at ease only in places of the world that conform to its norms of comfort and communication, but is more awkward than anyone else when dropped in the middle of deprived surroundings. Conversely, poor people used to adverse circumstances are better able to adapt to changing conditions of life and to face danger. The superiority of elites is largely a projection of their arrogance.

What is true, though, is that global elites are able to coordinate their efforts to defend their interests on a larger scale than ordinary people, social movements, or civil society organizations, and this is clearly to the disadvantage of the latter. For instance, companies undertook global activities for decades before workers' collective action started to reach out to other countries. It was therefore easy for companies to play off the interests of local workers against those of other countries, whereas doing so across plants in the same country was hampered by possible coalitions of workers across plants of the same company. For companies operating at the European level, for instance, the creation of a company committee to inform and consult with employees was officially encouraged (not mandated) only in a

1994 directive. True enough, there is an International Trade Union Confederation (created in 2006 by merging two world associations), which boasts descent from the First International and celebrated 150 years of global workers' association in 2014, but it makes no operational contribution to day-to-day bargaining, and primarily acts as a lobbying agency.

NGOs and civil society initiatives are also in great need of international coordination to increase their effectiveness and share ideas, and a lot of progress remains to be made in the domain of global coordination and information sharing. There are useful databases, such as one covering international NGOs by the Council of Europe[3] and one covering wellbeing and sustainability initiatives by Wikiprogress (initially launched by the OECD and now independent).[4] There are international gatherings of civil society initiatives, such as the World Social Forum, civil society events around the G20 meetings,[5] and a conference of international NGOs organized by the Council of Europe. International NGOs such as Oxfam, working on development aid, now tend to partner with local associations in order to better adapt their interventions to local needs and respect the dignity of aid recipients. There are also internet campaign platforms, such as Avaaz.org, MoveOn.org, and Change.org, which are incredibly efficient at gathering large numbers of signatures for petitions in a few hours.

In Chapter 5, the Self-Employed Women Association (SEWA) was described as an interesting Indian NGO promoting an ideal of dignity and empowerment and being very effective at the national level. This organization is part of an international network of similar NGOs, called WIEGO (Women in Informal Employment: Globalizing and Organizing), founded in 1997 and now active in more than fifty countries. In its manifesto, it proclaims: "No amount of social inclusion of the working poor will compensate for their exclusion

[3] http://coe-ngo.org/#/ingos.
[4] http://wikiprogress.org/.
[5] https://civil-20.org/.

from – or their inclusion on unfavorable terms in – economic opportunities, financial and product markets, and economic planning. And no amount of social inclusion of the working poor will compensate for their lack of economic power and economic rights." This network enhances the effectiveness of each member association by sharing experiences, providing technical and teaching support, helping promote their agenda in international policy forums, and collecting expertise from a group of international scholars. This type of network appears very promising for increasing the effectiveness of NGOs pursuing similar agendas in different countries. The example of WIEGO proves that international coordination is possible even for the most disadvantaged populations, such as female informal workers.

Sometimes international coordination of local initiatives is really crucial to make them powerful. For instance, the problem of climate change cannot be addressed locally. If one university campus decides to make great efforts at emissions reductions, what is the impact on global emissions? Either negligible, or even harmful, if the reduction of consumption of fossil fuels by this university leaves these fuels more accessible to consumers who are more sensitive to prices. But if all universities of the world decided to make a joint effort, this would be less negligible, and they could influence the politics of climate change mitigation. Unfortunately, such an international effort by universities does not seem to be happening for now. Coordination remains national at this stage,[6] which is odd given how easy it is for institutions of higher education to build international networks when it is about research. Ninety-one large cities from all continents, covering about 8 percent of the world population, have launched such an international coordination in the C40 network, and this is significant because of their proximity to governmental circles.

Universities and mayors can connect across national boundaries. What remains a serious obstacle for deprived people is the

---

[6] For instance, in the USA, Second Nature (http://secondnature.org/) gathers 589 (as of August 22, 2017) colleges and universities.

difficulty of communicating with large circles due to language constraints and limited access to networks. But this limitation becomes less and less of a handicap with modern technologies and the availability of civil society organizations and volunteers willing to help. For instance, the launch of SEWA in India has greatly benefited from the initiative of someone like Ela Bhatt, who came from a well-off family (her father was a lawyer, her mother an activist in women's associations) and was well educated and inspired by international experience. But once the initiative is set in place and helps to bridge gaps between deprived people, they invest in the structure and make it live on.

In conclusion, whenever possible, try to link with international initiatives similar to what you do and think of coordinated actions which amplify the impact of your action. And if you have the occasion to help coordinate less advantaged people who cannot easily communicate or access network, don't hesitate, while leaving the ultimate control of the initiative to them.

FIVE IDEAS THAT CAN CHANGE YOUR LIFE – AND THE WORLD

Now let us get concrete. Here are ideas about things that you can do to initiate social progress around you.

1. Bring Change Through Your Family

As emphasized in the introductory chapter, the situation of women remains far from perfect everywhere in the world, and we must continue and expand the change that has already been achieved. The education of girls, the health of women, and task sharing at home are three points where effort remains needed and for which everyone's contribution can make a difference. Depending on the context, this can take many different forms. In some places, sending girls to school is a heroic action, while in other places what remains to be done is to encourage girls to study in fields and prepare for occupations that have been monopolized by boys. It is very hard, in both sexes, to free oneself from stereotypes and to stop projecting on girls and women specific roles, but it is not impossible, and it is rewarding to see human beings get access to new things they have been artificially barred from. While women's and maternal health care is primarily a policy issue, it is also a family issue to let women have access to their fair share of food and comfort, to assist them in contraception efforts, and to encourage them to get the desirable level of health care.

Task sharing is an area in which progress is depressingly slow (IPSP 2018, chapter 17), producing a situation in which giving access to more work opportunities to women means overloading their day with multiple responsibilities. It is not just a matter of public policy, but also a matter of family negotiation, to force men to take more time with their children, to share more in cleaning and meal preparation and in the care of elderly relatives. Wherever you are, break rules and conventions that entrench inequalities.

Beyond the gender issue, there is also the question of sexual orientation and gender identity. The family is a key place where sexual orientation and gender identity can be respected or repressed, and it is therefore very important for family members to be open-minded and respectful of difference. A similar need for open minds and respect arises when romantic relations across religions or races break traditional conventions.

Don't believe that what happens in the family is not an issue of serious social justice. The family is one of the places of the most egregious injustices, and a strategic place where girls and women are either encouraged and prepared to take their place in society, or conditioned to remain in secondary roles; where differences in sexual orientation, race, or religions can be welcomed or suppressed, reflecting attitudes that foster or hinder the flourishing of differences in society at large. More fundamentally, the family is the first and most important form of cooperative behavior in human evolution, and still involves absolutely key power and distribution mechanisms that shape people's lives today. Your family can be an actor of change not just for your family members, but also as an example and inspiration for other families around yours.

2. Bring Change Through Your Work

The other place that shapes the deepest injustices is work. Work is a cooperative venture where different participants bring their know-how and their energy to produce something together and obtain a reward. At work there is not only a fight to share the proceeds, but also a fight for roles, standing, recognition, power, responsibility, and autonomy. Traditional hierarchies persist and divide workers into categories, and also separate workers from other contributors such as creditors and shareholders. As explained in Chapter 6, a just workplace would treat everyone as a partner, as a contributor to the collective venture.

It is easy to think that not much can be changed, in this respect, by individual or local initiative. Globalization has reinforced the feeling that decisions are made far away and above the heads of the ordinary workers. The downward trend in unionization in many countries leaves many workers quite powerless and voiceless.

However, change is not that hard to implement in some contexts. First, in small firms where it is easy to communicate, it is also easy for owners and for employees to discuss better arrangements. In general, small firms have lower union coverage, but studies in various countries suggest that working conditions and labor–management relations are better in small firms. "Human-size" organizations are naturally more favorable to flourishing, and whether one is a manager or an ordinary worker, pushing for improvements in workers' status is worth some effort. This is not meant to suggest that large firms are hopeless. As Dane Atkinson writes about his democratic scheme:

> This self-electing team model could work in almost any
> company. Larger organizations would need more people to play

intermediary roles like our VP of engineering,[7] but I would still cap team sizes at ten for the sake of communication. This model scales nicely because it creates a queue of experienced employees who can rise to the top of new teams and save current managers from becoming overburdened.

It is also possible for workers to recover their dignity by moving to other firms, or by becoming self-employed. This may not be easy for all, but those for whom it is easy may want to think twice about their current situation, where they may have some perks and material guarantees, but at the cost of deplorable social relations at work. Even if, and especially if, you are not a victim in a workplace that is full of unfair practices, you have a special responsibility to make things change or, if this is not possible, to express your disagreement by quitting. Watch out for firms with social and environmental purposes, cooperatives, and B corps, and encourage them by signaling your interest in joining them.

It is not normal to treat workers like inferior human beings, and norms are slowly changing by the joint efforts of the victims, social movements, civil society organizations, and entrepreneurs with a better vision. The workplace is also a key site where gender and race relations can be very unfair and can reinforce discrimination that occurs in society at large. While social relations at work are partly a matter of public policy, individual practices and initiatives can make a difference and change the lives of many workers.

Think of it. If you contribute to making your workplace fair, this is a central element of fairness in your life. No matter how unjust other workplaces may remain, at least your life is an example of what can be achieved in a better society.

---

[7] "The VP of engineering oversees multiple teams, so the whole company had to vote yay or nay before we could hire him."

3. *Bring Change Through Your Consumption and Savings Choices*

You can also change workplaces in your consumer decisions, and this gives leverage even to those who do not work. It unfortunately remains difficult for "ethical" consumers to obtain accurate and reliable information about products. The websites providing corporate social responsibility ratings remain arcane or expensive, and they are conceived more for companies seeking to benchmark their performance than for households. A few websites, and even mobile apps, provide consumer guidance about products, but it remains complicated to obtain a synthetic picture of a product or service. Assuming that such tools will expand and improve, relying on them can help you navigate the maze of labels and ads, and not only does it give you the satisfaction of consuming products which have been made in good conditions, it also makes you a contributor to the general good cause of incentivizing companies to improve their ratings in order to keep customers. Similarly, ethical investment funds make it possible for the ordinary household to put savings to good use, and again, influence companies by giving an edge to those that demonstrate the desired behavior.

Most people say that they are willing to make an effort, including a financial effort, to be ethical in their consumption and savings. What is needed is a real movement in favor of ethical consumption and investment that will trigger the emergence of a better supply of free data about the social and environmental performance of firms.

4. *Bring Change to Your Community*

This is where the "think global, act local" slogan remains valid. There are thousands of ways community life can be improved, and many sources of ideas about how to create occasions for social interaction, how to revitalize neighborhoods, how to grow food together in almost any setting, how to make life more sustainable. Simply participating in a local club contributes to maintaining community life and cohesion. There are also fascinating innovations. Among the many inspiring stories, let us just mention the Incredible Edible, a movement that started in 2008 in the little town of Todmorden, in England, and has now been implanted in many countries on all continents. These groups develop community life around the project of growing food locally, raising environmental consciousness and helping integrate various parts of the community. They often let people collect food freely, changing the relation between participation and work, and transforming people's vision of public spaces. Another important initiative is the network of Mother Centers, also spread throughout the world (in the United States, Germany, and the former socialist European countries, but also in countries like Rwanda and Cameroon), which provides basic services including child care, adult education classes, and retraining, and relies on the empowerment philosophy of making people participate and contribute instead of being passive recipients of aid (IPSP 2018a, chapter 5). Gawad Kalinga[8] is yet another interesting story. A community development foundation based initially in the Philippines, it has significantly contributed over the last ten years to the reduction of poverty in that region by empowering local actors and mobilizing global firms and organizations around the common project of nurturing the emergence of many local healthy, productive, and caring socio-economic communities.

Community life is not just about what people do in given settings but also about urban design and infrastructure. Participating in local decisions about urban planning affecting people's lodging, access to facilities, and mobility options can be very important as most investments shape neighborhood life for decades to come. There is an interesting development in participatory mechanisms, inspired partly by Porto Alegre and similar initiatives described in Chapter 8. One shortcoming of such initiatives is that they sometimes contribute

[8] www.gk1world.com/NewOurVision.

to dividing social groups further, between those who are engaged and able to influence decisions, and those who feel disenfranchised and not able to really get in. Therefore, it may be worthwhile not just to make an effort to participate but also to seek ways to encourage more people to participate, from different social groups. Associations often have vocal people who can then relay the message that participation is encouraged. Sometimes, action for a just city involves resisting urban renewal when such "renewal" erases mixed neighborhoods and reinforces segregation.

5. Be a Torch-Bearer

Many people now tend to obtain their news from social media and non-professional channels, generating a proliferation of sectarian views that see the world in distorted ways, often filled with imaginary stories and conspiracy theories. This makes people gullible and vulnerable to demagogues. As explained in Chapter 8, the ideal society would treat media information more as a public good than as a commercial product, providing free access to good-quality news. We are not yet in such an ideal world, and therefore everyone must make an effort to stay informed in a responsible way, which involves contributing to the financial survival of professional journalism and selecting sources of news in a careful way, seeking to simultaneously avoid state control, corporate influence, and sectarian sirens. Just staying reasonably well informed is now an act of militancy.

A new development has now appeared with the spread of new technologies of communication. People have now become contributors to the media in various ways. In particular, everyone equipped with a smartphone can watch out for events and record them on the spot in order to report them to suitable media outlets. This has been transformative in its undermining of the impunity of abusive people such as brutal police officers or rapists. The simple fact of a greater possibility of video proof of misdeeds is changing social norms. Of course, some people complain that this is a form of Big Brother surveillance, but overall we, and especially the most vulnerable among us, seem better off with a multiplication of graphical proofs of reprehensible acts.

More basically and importantly, one can also be a torchbearer by choosing the type and contents of education for oneself and one's children, making sure that it is not limited to fulfilling job qualifications but also endows the student with the civic and cultural competence that responsible citizens need in order to be able to understand how the world is going and where the common good lies.

BE AN ACTIVE CITIZEN

There is a sixth idea that deserves a separate section. Grassroots movements need to put pressure on governments and many changes must ultimately be enshrined in law. All the changes in corporate law, the welfare state, and political rules that have been presented in Chapters 6–8 require legal implementation. Transforming community life and urban design for greater justice involves local politics. And many of the changes that you can bring to your personal life, as described in the previous section, would be made easier with appropriate support from government services. Women's role in the family and in society can be enhanced with the help of suitable public services of education, health care, child care, and elderly care, as well as rules for gender-balanced parental leave, pay equality, parity in elective offices, and so on. Making labor relations more horizontal and democratic would be easier with legal requirements that would remove unfair competition based on exploiting workers. Better access to higher education and lifelong learning empowers workers and citizens in their lives. Community transformations can be fostered by public policies that encourage associations and set up participation mechanisms. A better media system would require strict regulation of media ownership and control to preserve the independence of professional journalism from state and corporate influence.

Being an active citizen can help in bringing about these legal changes, and in many countries nowadays politics is very volatile and can be moved by the action of popular movements and citizen initiative. But there is a serious difficulty. Many reforms can be enforced nationally. But some actions require, or at least would be made easier by, international coordination. Here are two examples.

Climate policy cannot really be initiated by one country, because it is a global problem and reducing emissions of greenhouse gases at the world level to a sufficient extent cannot be achieved by a single country. It is therefore important to promote international cooperation of all actors that can join hands across borders, and support the global efforts made by the United Nations Framework Convention on Climate Change. The Paris Agreement reached in 2015 is just an imperfect starting point; efforts need to be ramped up in the coming two decades, after which it will be too late to implement mitigation efforts in an effective and relatively costless way. The odds that the Paris Agreement will be sufficiently effective are small, unfortunately, and the joker that could save the world is technological progress. If green technologies become cheap sufficiently quickly, they could displace fossil fuels. However, public action in the form of research and taxes and subsidies can accelerate the technological transition. Citizen support for all such efforts is likely to be crucial in the coming years.

The other example for which coordination would be helpful is corporate governance. Democratic governance in the economy will not become the rule without legal constraints, as explained in Chapters 6 and 8. But national states are submitted to blackmail by companies threatening to move operations abroad if policies are not sufficiently business-friendly. Minimum wages, taxes, and competition and governance regulation can all be used by firms as arguments in the threat of capital flight. The OECD and the European Union have been slowly but increasingly taking these issues into due consideration. It is important for workers and democratically minded entrepreneurs to join forces at the global level and work together to impose new norms of conduct. The ILO has launched a "decent work" initiative that could support initiatives going in this direction, but the ILO alone is quite powerless at the current juncture.

A grassroots push from business, labor, social movements, and civil society organizations is needed.

BE OPEN AND ADAPTIVE

As has been repeatedly hammered home in this book, there is no single model, no single recipe for transformation. It is very important to adapt general principles of human dignity and needs to local contexts and possibilities, and to exclude all forms of dogmatism.

What is fascinating about the current period is the transition from an old world to a new world. Old-style parties and unions, as well as consumer coops, are on the decline. New forms of action are on the rise, and they include organizations and movements which are more fluid, more able to communicate and coordinate on a large scale, but also less fixed in institutional structure and less resilient to fluctuations in membership and interest. The new change-makers must be able to seize opportunities for new forms of action and new coalitions of actors.

Facing this complex world, many thinkers simply abandon the old ideas and principles of social justice and imagine that totally new causes have to be embraced. This is a big mistake. The causes of women, workers, and dominated ethnic groups, are still with us and should remain at the center of the effort for social progress, while sexual orientation and gender identity issues also deserve increasing attention. But the perspectives for a better society are new and involve new combinations of market mechanisms and other forms of social interactions and regulations. Working toward this new society is the exciting task of our generation and the ones to come.

Appendix: *Rethinking Society for the 21st Century: Report of the International Panel on Social Progress* – Table of Contents

Contributing Authors:
Gustaf Arrhenius • Tim Campbell • Simon Caney •
John Roemer

Socio-Economic Transformations

Chapter 3   Economic Inequality and Social
            Progress   83

Coordinating Lead Authors:
Stephan Klasen • Giovanni Andrea Cornia • Rebeca
Grynspan • Luis F. López-Calva • Nora Lustig

Lead Authors:
Augustin Fosu • Sripad Motiram • Flora Myamba •
Andreas Peichl • Sanjay Reddy • Eldar Shafir • Ana Sojo •
Ingrid Woolard

Contributing Authors:
Shai Davidai • Michael Förster • Rahul Lahoti • Judith
Sutz • Rainer Thiele

Chapter 4   Economic Growth, Human Development,
            and Welfare   141

Coordinating Lead Authors:
Purnamita Dasgupta • Ottmar Edenhofer

Lead Authors:
Adriana Mercedes Avendano Amezquita •
Antonio Bento • Simon Caney • David De la Croix •
Augustin Fosu • Michael Jakob • Marianne Saam •
Kristin Shrader-Frechette • John Weyant • Liangzhi You

Contributing Authors:
Gian Carlo Delgado-Ramos • Marcel J. Dorsch •
Christian Flachsland • David Klenert • Robert Lempert
• Justin Leroux • Kai Lessmann • Junguo Liu • Linus
Mattauch • Charles Perrings • Gregor Schwerhoff • Kristin
Seyboth • Jan Steckel • Jessica Strefler

Lead Authors:
Itty Abraham • Karin Aggestam • Alexander Bellamy •
Lars-Erik Cederman • Jerôme Ferret • Jean Baptiste
Jeangène Vilmer • Wilhelm Heitmeyer •
Angela Muvumba-Sellström • Laurie Nathan •
Hideaki Shinoda • Ekaterina Stepanova

Contributing Author:
Olga Odgers Ortiz

Lead Authors:
Göran Bolin • Julie Cohen • Gerard Goggin •
Marwan Kraidy • Koichi Iwabuchi • Kwang-Suk Lee •
Jack Qiu • Ingrid Volkmer • Herman Wasserman •
Yuezhi Zhao

Contributing Authors:
Olessia Koltsova • Inaya Rakhmani • Omar Rincón •
Claudia Magallanes-Blanco • Pradip Thomas

Coordinating Lead Authors:
Richard Bellamy • Wolfgang Merkel

Lead Authors:
Rajeev Bhargava • Juliana Bidadanure • Thomas
Christiano • Ulrike Felt • Colin Hay • Lily Lamboy •
Thamy Pogrebinschi • Graham Smith • Gayil Talshir •
Nadia Urbinati • Mieke Verloo

**VOLUME 3: TRANSFORMATIONS IN VALUES,
NORMS, CULTURES**

Authors:
Olivier Bouin • Marie-Laure Djelic • Marc Fleurbaey •
Ravi Kanbur • Elisa Reis

Transformations in Values, Norms, Cultures

Coordinating Lead Authors:
John Bowen • Will Kymlicka

Lead Authors:
Martin Hopenhayn • Takyiwaa Manuh • Abdul Raufu Mustapha

Contributing Authors:
Faisal Garba • Jan Willem Duyvendak

Lead Authors:
Pascale Allotey • Gustaf Arrhenius • Uli Beisel •
Melinda Cooper • Nir Eyal • Dan Hausman •
Wolfgang Lutz • Ole F. Norheim • Elizabeth Roberts •
Denny Vågerö

Contributing Author:
Karim Jebari

Coordinating Lead Authors:
Christiane Spiel • Simon Schwartzman

Lead Authors:
Marius Busemeyer • Nico Cloete • Gili Drori •
Lorenz Lassnigg • Barbara Schober •
Michele Schweisfurth • Suman Verma

Contributing Authors:
Bilal Bakarat • Peter Maassen • Rob Reich

Coordinating Lead Authors:
Akeel Bilgrami • Prabhat Patnaik

Lead Authors:
Faisal Devji • Michele Lamont • Ernesto Ottone •
James Tully • Nira Wickramasinghe •
Sue Wright

Concluding Chapters

Coordinating Lead Authors:
Nancy Folbre • Erik Olin Wright

Lead Authors:
Jenny Andersson • Jeff Hearn • Susan Himmelweit •
Andrew Stirling

Coordinating Lead Authors:
Matthew Adler • Helga Nowotny

Lead Authors:
Cary Coglianese • Sheila Jasanoff • Ravi Kanbur •
Brian Levy • Ole F. Norheim • Johan Schot • Simon
Schwartzman • Christiane Spiel • Shana Starobin

References

Acemoglu D., P. Restrepo 2017, "Robots and Jobs: Evidence from US Labor Markets," NBER Working Paper 23285, www.nber.org/papers/w23285.pdf.

Alvaredo F., L. Chancel, T. Piketty, E. Saez, G. Zucman 2018, *The World Inequality Report*, Cambridge, MA: Belknap Press.

Asian Development Bank 2012, *Outlook 2012. Confronting Rising Inequality in Asia*, Mandaluyong City, Philippines: Asian Development Bank, www.adb .org/sites/default/files/publication/29704/ado2012.pdf.

Askenazy P. 2016, *Tous rentiers!* Paris: Odile Jacob.

ATD 2013, "Extreme Poverty is Violence. Breaking the Silence. Searching for Peace," Revue Quart Monde Documents no. 20, Pierrelaye, France: ATD.

Atkinson A.B. 2015, *Inequality: What Can Be Done?* Cambridge, MA: Harvard University Press.

Ausubel J.H., A.S. Curry, I.K. Wernick 2015, "Reconsidering Resources: Matter, Labor, Information, and Capital in the Future Security Environment," Program for the Human Environment, The Rockefeller University, New York.

Autor D. 2010, *The Polarization of Job Opportunities in the U.S. Labor Market*, Washington, DC: The Center for American Progress and The Hamilton Project.

Autor D.H., D. Dorn, G.H. Hanson 2016, "The China Shock: Learning from Labor Market Adjustment to Large Changes in Trade," NBER Working Paper 21906.

Babb S. 2012, "The Washington Consensus as Transnational Policy Paradigm: Its Origins, Trajectory and Likely Successor," *Review of International Political Economy* 20(2): 268–297.

Balinski M., R. Laraki 2011, *Majority Judgement: Measuring, Ranking and Electing*, Cambridge, MA: MIT Press.

Barkai S. 2017, "Declining Labor and Capital Shares," London Business School, mimeo.

Bartels L. 2016, *Unequal Democracy: The Political Economy of the New Gilded Age*, 2nd edn, New York and Princeton, NJ: Russell Sage Foundation and Princeton University Press.

Brams S.J., P.C. Fishburn 1983, *Approval Voting*, Boston: Birkhauser.

Carney B.M., I. Getz 2016, *Freedom, Inc. How Corporate Liberation Unleashes Employee Potential and Enhances Business Performance*, 2nd edn, Somme Valley House.

Case A., A. Deaton 2015, "Rising Morbidity and Mortality in Midlife among White Non-Hispanics Americans in the 21st century," *PNAS*, 112(49): 15078–15083.

2017, "Mortality and Morbidity in the 21st Century," Brookings Papers on Economic Activity, BPEA Conference Drafts.

Casey G., O. Galor 2017, "Is Faster Economic Growth Compatible with Reductions in Carbon Emissions? The Role of Diminished Population Growth," *Environmental Research Letters* 12(1): 014003.

Collomb J.D. 2014, "The Ideology of Climate Change Denial in the United States," *European Journal of American Studies* 9(1): 1–17.

Corak M. 2013, "Income Inequality, Equality of Opportunity and Intergenerational Mobility," *Journal of Economic Perspectives* 27: 79–102.

Dahl R.A. 1961, *Who Governs? Democracy and Power in an American City*, New Haven, CT: Yale University Press.

2006, *On Political Equality*, New Haven, CT: Yale University Press.

Easterlin R.A., R. Morgan, M. Switek, Fei Wang 2012, "China's Life Satisfaction, 1990–2010," *Proceedings of the National Academy of Sciences* 109: 9775–9780.

Edenhofer O., B. Knopf, C. Bak, A. Bhattacharya 2017, "Aligning Climate Policy with Finance Ministers' G20 Agenda," *Nature Climate Change* 7: 463–465.

Edgerton D. 2006, *The Shock of the Old*, Oxford: Oxford University Press.

Esping-Andersen G. 1990, *The Three Worlds of Welfare Capitalism*, Cambridge: Polity.

European Commission 2010, *Social Protection for Inclusive Development. A New Perspective in EU Cooperation with Africa*, European Report on Development, Brussels: European Commission.

Ezrahi Y. 1990, *The Descent of Icarus: Science and the Transformation of Contemporary Democracy*, Cambridge, MA: Harvard University Press.

Foa R.S., Y. Mounk 2016, "The Democratic Disconnect," *Journal of Democracy* 27(3): 5–17.

Francis A.M., M. Tannuri-Pianto 2013, "Endogenous Race in Brazil: Affirmative Action and the Construction of Racial Identity among Young Adults," *Economic Development and Cultural Change* 61(4): 731–753.

Freeman R. 1984, *Strategic Management: A Stakeholder Approach*, Cambridge: Cambridge University Press.

Friedman M. 1970, "The Social Responsibility of Business is to Increase Its Profits," *The New York Times Magazine*, September 13.

Fukuyama F. 1992, *The End of History and the Last Man*, New York: Free Press.

Giddens A. 1998, *The Third Way: The Renewal of Social Democracy*, Cambridge, UK, and Malden, MA: Polity.

Goldstein J.S. 2011, *Winning the War on War: The Decline of Armed Conflict Worldwide*, New York: Penguin.

Graham C., S. Zhou, J. Zhang 2015, "Happiness and Health in China: The Paradox of Progress," Global Economy and Development Working Paper Series No. 89, Washington, DC: Brookings Institution.

Hallegatte S., M. Bangalore, L. Bonzanigo, M. Fay, T. Kane, U. Narloch, J. Rozenberg, D. Treguer, A. Vogt-Schilb 2016, *Shock Waves: Managing the Impacts of Climate Change on Poverty*, Washington, DC: World Bank.

Hayek F. 1944, *The Road to Serfdom*, Chicago: University of Chicago Press.

Held D. 2004, *Global Covenant. The Social Democratic Alternative to the Washington Consensus*, Cambridge, UK, and Malden, MA: Polity.

Huber E., J. Bogliaccini 2010, "Latin America," in *The Oxford Handbook of the Welfare State*, ed. F.G. Castles, S. Leibfried, J. Lewis, H. Obinger, C. Pierson, Oxford: Oxford University Press.

Hyung-sik Eum 2017, *Cooperatives and Employment. Second Global Report*, Geneva: CICOPA.

ILO 2017, *World Social Protection Report*, Geneva: ILO.

IPSP 2018a, *Rethinking Society for the 21st Century. Report of the International Panel on Social Progress, vol. 1: Socio-Economic Transformations*, Cambridge: Cambridge University Press.

   2018b, *Rethinking Society for the 21st Century. Report of the International Panel on Social Progress, vol. 2: Political Regulation, Governance, and Societal Transformations*, Cambridge: Cambridge University Press.

   2018c, *Rethinking Society for the 21st Century. Report of the International Panel on Social Progress, vol. 3: Transformations in Values, Norms, Cultures*, Cambridge: Cambridge University Press.

Jacques P.J., R.E. Dunlap, M. Freeman 2008, "The Organisation of Denial: Conservative Think Tanks and Environmental Scepticism," *Environmental Politics* 17(3): 349–385.

Jaworek M., M. Kuzel 2015, "Transnational Corporations in the World Economy. Formation, Development and Present Position," *Copernican Journal of Finance and Accounting* 4(1): 55–70.

Jensen M., W. Meckling 1976, "Theory of the Firm: Managerial Behavior, Agency Costs and Ownership Structure," *Journal of Financial Economics* 3(4): 305–360.

Kolstad I., A. Wiig 2016, "Does Democracy Reduce Corruption?" *Democratization* 23(7): 1198–1215.

Krippner G. 2005, "The Financialization of the American Economy," *Socio-Economic Review* 3(2): 173–208.

Lakner C., B. Milanovic 2015, "Global Income Distribution: From the Fall of the Berlin Wall to the Great Recession," *Revista de Economía Institucional* 17(32): 71–128.

Mazzucato, Mariana 2013, *The Entrepreneurial State: Debunking Public vs. Private Sector Myths*, London: Anthem Press.

McCulloch J.R. 1856, *Considerations on Partnerships with Limited Liability*, London: Longman, Brown, Green and Longmans.

Meade J.E. 1964, *Efficiency, Equality and the Ownership of Property*, London: Allen & Unwin.

Nesbit J. 2016, *Poison Tea: How Big Oil and Big Tobacco Invented the Tea Party and Captured the GOP*, New York: Macmillan.

OECD 2016, "Social Spending Stays at Historically High Levels in OECD Countries," Social Expenditure Update, Paris: OECD.

  2017, *Bridging the Gap: Inclusive Growth 2017 Update Report*, Paris: OECD.

O'Neill B.C., B. Liddle, L. Jiang, K.R. Smith, S. Pachauri, M. Dalton, R. Fuchs 2012, "Demographic Change and Carbon Dioxide Emissions," *Lancet* 380(9837): 157–164.

Palley T. 2013, *Financialization*, London: Palgrave MacMillan.

Pigou A.C. 1920, *The Economics of Welfare*, New York: Palgrave MacMillan.

Piketty T. 2014, *Capital in the 21st Century*, Cambridge, MA: Harvard University Press.

Piketty T., G. Zucman 2014, "Capital is Back: Wealth–Income Ratios in Rich Countries, 1700–2010," *Quarterly Journal of Economics* 129(3): 1255–1310.

Piketty T., E. Saez, G. Zucman 2016, "Distributional National Accounts: Methods and Estimates for the United States," NBER Working Paper 22945.

Pinker S. 2011, *The Better Angels of Our Nature: Why Violence has Declined*, New York: Viking.

Polanyi K. 1944, *The Great Transformation*, New York: Farrar and Rinehart.

Reeves R.V. 2017, *Dream Hoarders: How the American Upper Middle Class Is Leaving Everyone Else in the Dust, Why That Is a Problem, and What to Do About It*, Washington, DC: Brookings Institution Press.

Reich R. 2015, *Saving Capitalism*, New York: Vintage.

Salmi J. 2017, *The Tertiary Education Imperative. Knowledge, Skills and Values for Development*, Rotterdam: Springer.

Sandel M. 2013, *What Money Can't Buy: The Moral Limits of Markets*, London: Penguin.

Satz D. 2010, *Why Some Things Should Not Be For Sale*, Oxford: Oxford University Press.

Sen A. 1981, *Poverty and Famines: An Essay on Entitlement and Deprivation*, Oxford: Oxford University Press.

Sinn H.W. 2010, *Casino Capitalism: How the Financial Crisis Came About and What Needs to be Done Now*, New York: Oxford University Press.

Smith A. 2012 [1776], *An Inquiry into the Nature and Causes of the Wealth of Nations*, Chicago: University of Chicago Press.

Springmann M., H.C.J. Godfray, M. Rayner, P. Scarborough 2016, "Analysis and Valuation of the Health and Climate Change Cobenefits of Dietary Change," *PNAS* 113(12): 4146–4151.

Stern N., J.E. Stiglitz 2017, *Report of the High-Level Commission on Carbon Prices*, Washington, DC: Carbon Pricing Leadership Coalition.

Stiglitz J.E. 2015, *Rewriting the Rules of the American Economy*, New York: Roosevelt Institute.

Stout L. 2012, *The Shareholder Value Myth*, Oakland, CA: Berrett-Koehler.

Telles E. 2004, *Race in Another America: The Significance of Skin Color in Brazil*, Princeton, NJ: Princeton University Press.

UNRISD 2016, *Policy Innovations for Transformative Change. Implementing the 2030 Agenda for Sustainable Development*, Geneva: UNRISD.

Van Benthem A.A. 2015, "Energy Leapfrogging," *JEARE* 2(1): 93–132.

Van Parijs P., Y. Vanderborght 2017, *Basic Income. A Radical Proposal for a Free Society and a Sane Economy*, Cambridge, MA: Harvard University Press.

Von Neumann J. 1955, "Can We Survive Technology?" *Fortune Editors* January 13, 2013, http://fortune.com/2013/01/13/can-we-survive-technology/.

Weber M. 2001, *The Protestant Ethic and the Spirit of Capitalism*, first pub. 1904, New York: Taylor & Francis.

World Bank 2017, *Governance and the Law*, World Development Report, Washington, DC: World Bank.

2018, *Distributional Tensions and A New Social Contract*, Washington, DC: World Bank.

Wright E.O., R.E. Dwyer 2017, "A Half-Century of Job Growth: From Upgrading to Polarization in the American Jobs Structure from the 1960s to the 2010s," unpublished manuscript.

Index